Sommeliers' Heaven

Sommeliers' Heaven

Paolo Basso
Best Sommelier of the World

THE GREATEST WINE CELLARS OF THE WORLD

BRAUN

CONTENTS

For those special moments ...

The Italian-Swiss sommelier Paolo Basso was born in 1966 in Besnate in Lombardy. He completed his professional training at the Italian Hotel Management School in Sondalo and the Swiss Sommelier Association School. In 2010 he was named as Best Sommelier of Europe ASI, and in 2013 as Best Sommelier of the World ASI. He is a leading specialist for special and rare wines. In this preface, he describes his emotional and professional relationship to the world of wine.

Nature

In my eyes grapes are a gift from the earth and it is the skill of transforming these gifts into wine that has always fascinated me. Depending on natural conditions, the composition of the soil, the knowledge and skills of the oenologist and the quality of the cellar; wine can be stored for years, until the perfect moment arrives in which to enjoy it.

Wine Cellar

Even as a small boy I was fascinated by wine. My grandfather had a cellar that we were forbidden to enter as children. The only time this ban was lifted was during the grape harvest, when we were also permitted to participate in the hustle and bustle. It was probably the attraction of the forbidden that causes me even now to experience a wine cellar as a secret and magical place.

Decision

After attending a hotel management school, where I was mostly interested in the subject "Food and Beverages", I worked in a restaurant and was lucky enough to make the acquaintance of a regular customer who was a wine enthusiast and connoisseur. He generously shared his knowledge, his love of wine, and even the precious wines themselves. In return for his generosity we impressed him with our enthusiasm and passion. It was this meeting that intensified my love of wine and indirectly encouraged me to dedicate my life to studying this subject.

Sommelier

These days, the profession of sommelier is extremely varied. It comprises not only serving wine to guests, but also managing the wine cellar, which must always meet the customers' needs and demands. In other words, this involves buying wine that

appeals to customers. It must be possible to sell the wines efficiently in order to avoid having bottles that remain indefinitely in the cellar. The only exceptions to this rule are the really excellent wines that are stored in the cellar for years and left to mature. These are truly precious...

Know-How

As the 'manager' of a wine cellar, one has to always be aware of the responsibility that comes with purchasing wine, as this costs a restaurant, hotel or vinotheque a considerable amount of money. Equally, a certain measure of psychological sensitivity is indispensable, because there is little time to advise guests and gather the answers to the following important questions. Is the guest a wine connoisseur? Or is he in the process of taking his first tentative steps into the fascinating world of wine? Is he ready to enjoy an exquisite wine or would he rather try a good but less expensive wine? Does he tend to allow his choices to be guided by the selection of wines on the menu or would he rather make up his own mind?

Architecture

Architects and sommeliers share an unspoken sense of beauty and perfection. As part of a harmonious interaction, architects give the wine the opportunity to mature in a fantastic setting. The sommelier carries the responsibility of providing the perfect ambience for serving or selling the wine.

Storage

The wine cellar is the place that provides the perfect conditions for the wine to mature and unfold. The optimal interaction between temperature, humidity, darkness and natural daylight is essential for storing the best wines, which only reach their full potential after a few years or even decades.

Moment

I love the idea that a wine has been kept specifically for this special moment of enjoyment, and the knowledge that it will be drunk at the right moment when it is fully mature. This is also true of the more 'simple' wines, those that give the day that special something. Whether accompanying an evening meal with the family or an evening with friends – for me, wine is the epitome of culture and happiness.

Tasting

External conditions determine whether my relationship to wine is characterized by professionalism or emotion. At professional tastings and when reviewing wine, I make use of my own personal method that I have perfected and developed based on French, Italian and English tasting methods.

Curiosity

A sommelier must maintain a certain childish curiosity and openness. Evolving from my desire to broaden my knowledge, I spend a considerable amount of my spare time reading books and magazines about oenology, and about dining culture in general – mineral water, coffee, tea and spirits.

Private Life

An intrinsic aspect of a profession that is both a job and a hobby, is that the work of a sommelier doesn't finish at the end of the working day; a sommelier's private life is also defined by his passion for wine. If I drink wine with friends or with my family, I can't avoid evaluating it; although the occasion, environment and the atmosphere of the moment are of course paramount.

My Daughter

I have finally been able to fulfill my dream of producing my own wine. I have dedicated it to my daughter Chiara and her red hair, which was the main inspiration for the name: "Il Rosso di Chiara", which translates as "The red of Chiara". The wine is a blend of Merlot, Cabernet Sauvignon und Cabernet Franc. The grapes were picked and processed in Mendrisiotto, in the Canton of Ticino.

Pour cet instant d'exception...

Paolo Basso est né à Besnate (Lombardie) en 1966. Ce sommelier italo-suisse est diplômé de l'École d'hôtellerie de Sondalo (Italie) et de l'Association de la sommellerie internationale de Lugano (Suisse), qui l'a élu Meilleur sommelier d'Europe en 2010 et Meilleur sommelier du monde en 2013. Comptant parmi les plus grands spécialistes en matière de vins rares, il parle ci-dessous de ses rapports affectifs et professionnels au monde du vin.

La nature

Le raisin est à mes yeux un cadeau de la terre. J'ai toujours été fasciné par la capacité des vignerons à le transformer en vin. Résultat des conditions naturelles qui règnent dans le vignoble, du savoir-faire des vignerons et de la qualité des caves, le vin peut mûrir durant des décennies, attendant patiemment l'instant propice pour être dégusté.

La cave

Le vin exerce sur moi une fascination extraordinaire depuis ma plus tendre enfance. Mon grand-père avait une cave à laquelle nous n'avions pas accès lorsque nous étions petits, sauf durant les vendanges, période de grande activité vinicole. C'est sûrement du fait de cet interdit que les caves à vin restent pour moi des lieux mystérieux et magiques jusqu'à l'heure actuelle.

La décision

J'avais choisi la spécialité « Alimentation et boissons » durant ma formation à l'école d'hôtellerie. Ultérieurement, alors que je travaillais dans un restaurant, j'eus la chance de faire la connaissance d'un client régulier, grand amateur de vins fins, qui nous fit partager son savoir et son amour pour le bon vin. Il nous donna souvent l'occasion d'en goûter, suscitant en nous un enthousiasme qui le réjouissait. Ce contact eut pour conséquence de développer ma passion pour le vin, ce qui m'amena de manière indirecte à y consacrer ma vie.

Le sommelier

Le travail d'un sommelier est très varié de nos jours. Il ne consiste pas uniquement à servir le vin, mais aussi à gérer une cave en l'adaptant aux attentes de la clientèle. En d'autres termes, le sommelier doit savoir discerner les crus qui se vendent le mieux afin d'éviter que des bouteilles restent trop longtemps dans la cave. Ce qui ne vaut évidemment pas pour les vins d'exception qui demandent, par contre, de mûrir lentement et que je considère personnellement comme de véritables trésors.

Le savoir-faire

Étant chargé de la gestion de la cave, le sommelier a une lourde responsabilité puisque l'achat du vin représente un budget considérable pour le propriétaire de l'hôtel, du restaurant ou de la vinothèque. De plus, il doit être fin psychologue lorsqu'il conseille les clients car il n'a que quelques instants pour répondre à diverses questions : le client est-il fin connaisseur ou débutant dans le monde fascinant du vin ? Est-il prêt à mettre le prix pour savourer un cru d'exception ou recherche-t-il plutôt un vin à meilleur marché ? Souhaite-t-il des conseils quant au menu ou va-t-il l'adapter lui-même au vin choisi ?

L'architecture

Architectes et sommeliers partagent le même goût pour le beau et la perfection : les premiers créent des espaces dans lesquels le vin peut mûrir en bénéficiant de conditions idéales ; les seconds ont en charge de servir et vendre le vin de manière professionnelle dans les merveilleux espaces mis à leur disposition.

Le stockage

La cave est l'endroit où le vin, stocké dans des conditions idéales, peut mûrir en toute tranquillité. L'optimisation de facteurs tels que la température, l'humidité, la pénombre et l'éclairage artificiel est indispensable pour que les grands crus développent tout leur potentiel, ce processus pouvant s'étirer sur des années, voire des décennies.

L'instant

J'aime à penser qu'un vin est mis de côté pour un instant d'exception et qu'il sera bu lorsqu'il sera arrivé à maturité. Cela vaut pour les grands crus comme pour les vins de tous les jours qui confèrent un charme particulier à notre quotidien. Qu'il soit savouré lors d'un dîner en famille ou durant une soirée entre amis, le vin est toujours pour moi synonyme de joie et de savoir-vivre.

La dégustation

Mon rapport aux vins associe professionnalisme et sensibilité personnelle en fonction des conditions du moment. Lorsque je goûte un vin en tant qu'œnologue professionnel, je le fais selon une procédure « de mon cru » basée sur la méthode développée par des goûteurs français, italiens et anglais, méthode perfectionnée par mes soins.

La curiosité

Un sommelier doit savoir garder une certaine dose de la curiosité et de l'ouverture d'esprit typiques de l'enfance. Toujours attaché à approfondir mes connaissances en la matière, je passe beaucoup de temps à lire des livres et des magazines consacrés non seulement au vin mais aussi aux arts de la table, au café, au thé, aux spiritueux et à l'eau minérale.

La vie privée

Le sommelier, dont le métier est aussi un violon d'Ingres, exerce son activité avec passion même après avoir quitté son lieu de travail. Lorsque je bois du vin en famille ou avec des amis, je ne saurais m'empêcher de le goûter et de l'analyser. Je garde néanmoins mes impressions pour moi car le cadre et l'atmosphère générale de l'événement sont alors de nature purement privée.

La fille

Après de nombreuses années, j'ai enfin pu réaliser mon rêve : produire mon propre vin, baptisé « Il Rosso di Chiara » en l'honneur de ma fille et de ses cheveux roux. Élaboré à partir de cépages Merlot, Cabernet Sauvignon et Cabernet Franc, ce vin est un pur produit du vignoble de Mendrisiotto, dans le Tessin méridional.

9

Für diesen ganz bestimmten Augenblick ...

Der italienisch-schweizerische Sommelier Paolo Basso wurde 1966 in Besnate in der Lombardei geboren. Er absolvierte Ausbildungen an der italienischen Hotel Management School in Sondalo und der Schweizer Sommelier Association School. 2010 wurde er zum Best Sommelier of Europe ASI gekürt, 2013 gar zum Best Sommelier of the World ASI. Er ist einer der führenden Spezialisten für besondere und seltene Weine. In diesem Vorwort beschreibt er seine emotionale und professionelle Beziehung zur Welt des Weines.

Die Natur

In meinen Augen sind Trauben ein Geschenk der Erde; die Fähigkeit von uns Menschen, diese Gaben in kostbaren Wein zu verwandeln, fasziniert mich seit jeher. Den Naturgegebenheiten, der Bodenbeschaffenheit, den Kenntnissen und Fähigkeiten des Önologen und der Kellerqualität entsprechend, kann der Wein jahrzehntelang im Keller ruhen, bis wir beschließen, dass der Moment gekommen ist, ihn zu genießen.

Der Weinkeller

Schon als kleiner Knabe übte Wein auf mich eine außerordentliche Faszination aus. Mein Großvater hatte einen Keller, dessen Zutritt uns Kindern untersagt war. Einzige Ausnahme des „Kellerverbotes" war die Zeit der Weinlese, in der auch wir am regen Treiben teilnehmen durften. Es wird wohl am ewigen Reiz des Verbotenen liegen, dass ich Weinkeller bis heute als geheimnisvolle und magische Orte empfinde.

Der Entschluss

Nach der Hotelfachschule, auf der mein Interesse insbesondere dem Fach „Ernährung und Getränke" galt, wurde mir während meiner Arbeit im Restaurant das Glück zuteil, die Bekanntschaft eines Stammkunden zu machen, der ein großer Weinkenner und -liebhaber war. Großzügig teilte er sein Wissen, seine Freude am Wein und auch die kostbaren Weine mit uns. Im Gegenzug erfreuten wir ihn durch unsere Begeisterung und unseren Enthusiasmus. Er war es, durch den sich meine Liebe zum Wein intensivierte und der mich indirekt dazu bewog, mein Leben dem Studium dieser Materie zu widmen.

Der Sommelier

Der Beruf des Sommeliers ist heutzutage sehr vielseitig. Er besteht nicht nur darin, den Gästen Wein auszuschenken, sondern schließt darüber hinaus die Verwaltung des Weinkellers mit ein, den es auf die Bedürfnisse der Kundschaft anzupassen gilt. Mit anderen Worten umfasst dies den Einkauf von Weinen, welche unter den Gästen möglichst großen Anklang finden. Sie müssen sich effizient weiterverkaufen lassen, sodass „Nesthocker" im Keller vermieden werden. Einzige Ausnahme sind die ausgezeichneten Weine, welche über Jahre im Keller lagern und reifen können und die ich ganz im Gegenteil als wertvolle Schätze bezeichne...

Das Know-How

Als „Verwalter" des Weinkellers muss man sich seiner großen Verantwortung beim Einkauf stets vollauf bewusst sein, da dieser für das Restaurant, das Hotel oder die Vinothek einen erheblichen Kostenpunkt darstellt. Ebenso ist für Sommeliers sein psychologisches Feingefühl unabdingbar, da bei der Beratung der Gäste nur wenige Augenblicke für die Beantwortung folgender Fragen bleiben: Ist der Gast ein Weinkenner oder unternimmt er gerade seine ersten Schritte in der fesselnden Welt der Weine? Ist er bereit, einen exquisiten Wein zu genießen oder wünscht er lieber einen guten, doch weniger teuren Wein? Ist er geneigt, sich bei der Wahl des Weines zum gewählten Menu leiten zu lassen oder trifft er lieber seine eigene Wahl?

Die Architektur

Architekten und Sommeliers teilen einen ausgesprochenen Sinn für Schönheit und Perfektion. In einer harmonischen Wechselbeziehung erfüllt der Architekt die Aufgabe, dem Wein die Möglichkeit zu geben, in einer traumhaften Umgebung zu reifen. Der Sommelier trägt die Verantwortung, diesen schließlich in einem schönen Ambiente professionell zu servieren oder zu verkaufen.

Die Lagerung

Der Weinkeller ist der Ort, an dem der ruhende Wein die idealen Gegebenheiten vorfindet, um reifen und sich entfalten zu können. Das optimale Zusammenspiel von Temperatur, Feuchtigkeit, Dunkelheit und Tageslichtbeleuchtung ist besonders für die Lagerung der „großen" Weine unentbehrlich, welche erst nach einigen Jahren oder Jahrzehnten ihr volles Potenzial offenbaren.

Der Moment

Ich liebe den Gedanken, dass der Wein für diesen ganz bestimmten Augenblick des Genusses aufbewahrt wurde und das Bewusstsein, dass er im richtigen Moment seiner Reife getrunken wird. Dies schließt auch die „einfacheren" Weine ein, welche dem Alltag seinen besonderen Glanz verleihen. Ob beim vertrauten Abendessen mit der Familie oder an einem Abend im Kreis der Freunde – Wein bedeutet für mich Kultur und Freude.

Die Verkostung

Ob mein Verhältnis zum Wein durch Professionalität oder Emotion geprägt ist, bestimmen die äußeren Umstände. Bei professionellen Verkostungen und Bewertungen von Weinen wende ich ein persönlich entwickeltes Verfahren an, welches ich auf der Basis der französischen, italienischen und englischen Verkostungsmethoden erarbeitet und perfektioniert habe.

Die Neugier

Ein Sommelier muss sich stets eine gewisse kindliche Neugierde und Aufgeschlossenheit bewahren. Von dem Wunsch geleitet, mich in die Materie zu vertiefen und mein Wissen auszubauen, verbringe ich viele Stunden meiner Freizeit damit, Bücher und Zeitschriften über Weinkunde, aber auch über die Tischkultur generell, Mineralwasser, Kaffee, Tee und Spirituosen zu lesen.

Das Privatleben

Als eine Profession, die Beruf und Hobby vereint, ist die Tätigkeit des Sommeliers nach Feierabend noch lange nicht beendet; auch das Privatleben ist durch die Leidenschaft geprägt. Wenn ich mit meiner Familie oder im Freundeskreis Wein trinke, komme ich nicht umhin, ihn für mich ganz persönlich zu bewerten, doch stehen Anlass, Umfeld und Atmosphäre des Moments klar im Vordergrund.

Die Tochter

Endlich habe ich meinen Traum verwirklichen können, meinen eigenen Wein zu produzieren. Gewidmet habe ich ihn meiner Tochter Chiara und ihren roten Haaren, welche bei der Namensgebung ausschlaggebend waren: „Il Rosso di Chiara", übersetzt „Der Rote von Chiara". Es handelt sich um einen Blend von Merlot, Cabernet Sauvignon und Cabernet Franc. Die Trauben werden im Mendrisiotto, einer Region des Tessins, gelesen und verarbeitet.

Architect | Fran Silvestre Arquitectos
Interior design | Alfaro Hofmann
Location | Carrer de Colón 37, 46004 Valencia, Spain
Year of completion | 2014
Client | Vegamar Selección
Type of venue | retail
Type of wine | Vegamar Selección
Number of seating places | 22
Trained sommelier | yes
Own vineyard | yes
Storage quality | ★★★☆☆

VEGAMAR SELECCIÓN WINE SHOP
Valencia, Spain

The Vegamar Selección wine shop is located on the town's main shopping street and offers space for wine tasting and sales. In order to emphasize the importance of the products, dark, glossy panels have been chosen for the vertical surfaces. The shiny surfaces of the panels help to blur the spatial limits of the establishment, making it seem bigger than it really is. This optical illusion is continued at the back of the wine bar, where backlit furniture and a large mirrored surface also give the impression of never ending space.

Cette vinothèque avec salle de vente et de dégustation est située dans la principale rue marchande de Valence. Les murs sont pourvus de panneaux anthracite brillants afin de mettre en valeur les bouteilles proposées à la vente et d'agrandir visuellement un espace somme toute assez restreint. Le long miroir et les meubles rétro-éclairés placés derrière le bar génèrent une illusion d'optique similaire.

Der Weinladen Vegamar Selección befindet sich inmitten des Einkaufsviertels von Valencia und bietet Räumlichkeiten für Weinproben und Verkauf. Um die Wertigkeit des Produkts zu betonen, wurden alle vertikalen Oberflächen mit dunklen, glänzenden Paneelen verkleidet. Die reflektierenden Oberflächen verwischen die Grenzen des Raumes zusätzlich, was ihn größer erscheinen lässt. Dies wird durch die am Ende des Raumes angeordnete Weinbar weiter verstärkt, deren durchgehende, von hinten beleuchtete Rückwand sich in den glänzenden Oberflächen spiegelt.

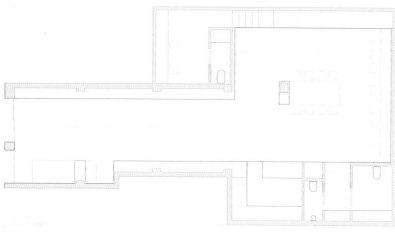

Architect | Focus Wine Cellars
Location | Ho Man Tin Hill, Kowloon, Hong Kong, China
Year of completion | 2012
Client | confidential
Type of venue | private wine cellar
Type of wine | mainly Bordeaux
Number of seating places | none, short tastings around the table
Cooling and ventilation techniques | Fondis purpose-built wine cellar air-conditioners
Storage quality | ★★★★☆

HO MAN TIN CELLAR
Hong Kong, China

The owners of this cellar are wine enthusiasts who allocated two rooms for use as a stunning wine cellar. Inspired by these two rooms, the cellar is organized as a narrative of spaces that flow into one another. From the entrance all the way to the wine safe at the end, the visitors are guided and amazed by intricate details, such as the polished tree trunk and hand-forged iron door. Since the owner is keen to purchase and display large bottles, all displays including special white leather-clad and CNC-cut glass shelves have been resized to better suit their purpose. Furthermore, all drawers are equipped with shelving that can be easily adjusted to accommodate bottles of varying sizes.

Le propriétaire d'un appartement de grand luxe du quartier de Ho Man Tin y a réservé deux pièces contiguës pour sa cave à vin. En allant de l'entrée vers le « coffre-fort à bouteilles », on découvre une multitude de détails sophistiqués, notamment un tronc d'arbre poli et une porte en fer forgé. Des étagères garnies de cuir blanc, découpées dans du verre à l'aide d'une machine CNC, ont été conçues spécialement pour présenter les magnums dont le propriétaire raffole. Quant aux différents tiroirs, ils sont pourvus d'étagères mobiles permettant de les adapter à tous les types de bouteilles.

Die Weinliebhaber stellten für ihren Weinkeller zwei der Wohnräume zur Verfügung, die als Abfolge von ineinanderfließenden Räumen gestaltet wurden. So begleiten den Besucher auf seinem Weg vom Eingang zum Weinsafe eine Fülle an beeindruckenden und faszinierenden Details wie ein polierter Baumstumpf oder eine handgeschmiedete eiserne Tür. Die Regalelemente bestehen aus CNC-gefrästen Glasböden mit einer Verkleidung aus weißem Leder, die, da sich der Eigentümer auf den Einkauf von Magnumflaschen spezialisiert hat, jeweils individuell angepasst wurden. Darüber hinaus wurden alle Schubladen mit variablen Halterungen ausgestattet, die verschiedene Flaschengrößen aufnehmen können.

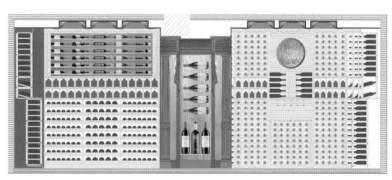

18

BODEGAS YSIOS WINERY
Laguardia, Spain

Architect | Santiago Calatrava
Location | Camino de la Hoya, 01300 Laguardia, Spain
Year of completion | 2001
Client | Bodegas and Bebidas Group
Type of venue | winery
Type of wine | reserve wines, unique blends
Storage quality | ★ ★ ★ ★ ★

The Bodegas and Bebidas Group wanted a building that would be an icon for its prestigious new wine "La Rioja Alavesa". Two 196-meter-long concrete, load-bearing walls have been placed parallel to each other and trace a sinusoidal shape in both plan and elevation. The southern façade is clad with horizontally placed cedar slats that create a strong contrast to the aluminum roof paneling. The façade to the north comprises precast concrete panels with few narrow openings. The eastern and western façades are clad in aluminum plates. In the center of the building the roof protrudes in a continuous volume over the visitors center that is conceived as a balcony overlooking the winery and the vineyards.

Le groupe Bodegas & Bebidas souhaiter faire construire un bâtiment digne de sa dernière cuvée, baptisée « La Rioja Alavesa ». Les architectes ont donc conçu une structure composée de deux murs porteurs longs de 196 mètres, caractérisés par leurs ondulations aussi bien sur le plan qu'en élévation. La façade sud est recouverte de shingles en cèdre disposés horizontalement qui contrastent fortement avec le toit en aluminium. La façade nord est en panneaux de béton préfabriqués percés seulement de quelques fenêtres étroites. À l'est et à l'ouest, finalement, le bâtiment est recouvert de plaques d'aluminium. Le toit s'élève au centre du bâtiment, au-dessus de l'accueil des visiteurs, pour former un belvédère dominant le vignoble.

Für ihren neuen hochwertigen Wein „La Rioja Alavesa" wollte die Bodegas und Bebidas Gruppe ein neues Wahrzeichen errichten lassen. Dazu wurden zwei 196 Meter lange, tragende Betonwände parallel zueinander platziert, die in horizontaler wie vertikaler Ausrichtung einer sinusförmigen Welle folgen. Die Südfassade wurde mit horizontalen Zedernlamellen verkleidet, die einen starken Kontrast zu der Aluminium-verkleidung des Daches bilden. Aluminiumplatten kamen auch als Verkleidung der Ost- und Westfassade zum Einsatz, während die Nordfassade aus vorgefertigten Betonplatten mit wenigen kleinen Fensteröffnungen besteht. In der Mitte des Gebäudes überwölbt das weit hervorragende Dach ein Besucherzentrum, welches weite Ausblicke über das Weingut und die Weinfelder ermöglicht.

Architect | Ippolito Fleitz Group
Location | Main-Taunus-Zentrum, 65843 Sulzbach, Germany
Year of completion | 2011
Client | Weinkellerei Höchst GmbH
Type of venue | retail
Storage quality | ★★★☆☆

WEIN & WAHRHEIT
Sulzbach, Germany

Weinkellerei Höchst has opened a second wine shop in the Main-Taunus shopping mall. Resembling a library of learned tomes, wine bottles fill the store from floor to ceiling along all three interior walls. A mirrored ceiling band running around the edges of the space further multiplies this effect in the vertical. Within the mirrored ceiling a canopy of glass vessels is suspended, forming a strong key visual. The light breaks in them like candlelight reflected through a glass, giving this otherwise modern setting the atmosphere of a wine cellar and conjuring up associations of epicurean indulgence. Glass and oak are the dominant materials in the space, both chosen to reference the world of wine. Their use results in a sensual ambience that appeals directly to the epicurean shopper.

Avec ses étagères montant jusqu'au plafond, le nouveau magasin de vente du vignoble Höchst ouvert dans le centre commercial Main-Taunus n'est pas sans évoquer une bibliothèque. Une bande de miroirs disposée sur le pourtour du plafond renforce encore cette impression en accentuant la verticalité. D'innombrables carafes suspendues à une toile accrochée au plafond constituent le clou de la décoration : la lumière s'y reflète comme les bougies dans les verres lorsqu'on savoure un bon vin, ce qui confère une atmosphère distinctement conviviale à cet espace au design moderne. Les architectes ont fait ici un large usage du verre et du bois de chêne, deux matériaux intimement connotés au monde du vin, qui formulent comme une invitation à l'épicurisme.

Die zweite Dependance der Weinkellerei Höchst gleicht einer Bibliothek erlesener Weine. Wie eine Bibliothek ist die Weinhandlung allseitig raumhoch mit Regalen versehen. Ein am Rand der Decke verlaufendes Spiegelband verstärkt den Effekt und vergrößert die Raumhöhe optisch. Unterhalb der verspiegelten Decke schwebt ein Segel, an dem einzelne Glaskörper aufgehängt sind, welche ein starkes Erkennungsmerkmal bilden. Sie brechen das Licht wie ein Glas bei Kerzenschein, und verleihen dem modernen Raum so eine Weinkelleratmosphäre, die man mit Lust am Genuss assoziiert. Dominierende Materialien sind Glas und Eiche, beide fest verwurzelt in der Welt des Weines. Sie bilden ein sinnliches Ambiente, das Genussmenschen direkt anspricht.

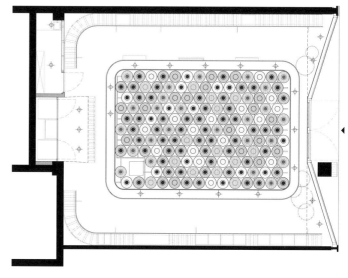

Architect | Carles Sala from Sala Ferusic Architects
Construction manager | Josep Maria Estivill
Location | Carreterra de Sant Pere Sacarrera a Sant Joan de Mediona, 08773 Barcelona, Spain
Year of completion | 2008
Client | Mas Rodó Vitivinícola
Type of venue | winery
Type of wine | Montonega, Macabeo, Riesling, Merlot, Cabernet Sauvignon
Number of seating places | 30
Cooling and ventilation techniques | ventilated wooden lightweight façade
Trained sommelier | yes
Own vineyard | yes
Storage quality | ★★★★★

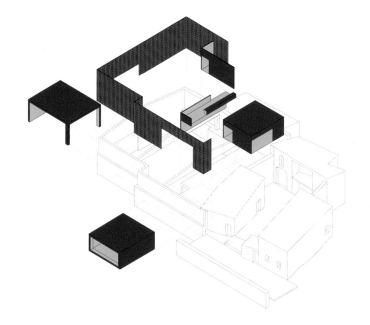

MAS RODÓ WINERY / SPRING IN PANTONE 375 C
Barcelona, Spain

The buildings of the Mas Rodó winery from the 18th century have been refurbished and transformed from a warehouse into a winery. Over an original masonry, a new wooden and steel façade redefines the volume. The double-skin façade helps to regulate the temperature inside the building, optimizing conditions for fermentation and minimizing energy consumption. The thickness of the old stone walls maintain the desired temperature. A large projecting window has been cut into the volume housing the tasting area, this is covered with corten steel and frames stunning views of the vineyards.

Le Mas Rodó, une ferme construite au XVIIIe siècle, a été récemment reconverti en vignoble. Le bâti d'origine se complète désormais d'extensions en bois et acier qui redéfinissent le volume de l'ensemble. Tout comme les anciens murs en pierre, la double enveloppe des nouveaux bâtiments permet de réguler la température de manière à optimiser les conditions de fermentation tout en minimisant la consommation d'énergie. La salle de dégustation s'ouvre par un grand oriel bardé d'acier Corten qui offre une vue magnifique sur le paysage environnant.

Die landwirtschaftlichen Lagerhäuser des Weinguts Mas Rodó aus dem 18. Jahrhundert wurden zu einem Weinkeller umgenutzt. Zur Neudefinition der Gebäudevolumen wurde das historische Mauerwerk mit einer Holz- und Stahlfassade überformt. Die doppelte Gebäudehülle reguliert die Temperatur im Inneren des Gebäudes, optimiert die Klimabedingung für den Fermentationsprozess und spart Energie. Die Dicke der alten Steinmauern hält die richtige Temperatur. Im Verkostungsbereich wurde ein großes Panoramafenster in die Gebäudehülle geschnitten und mit Cortenstahl eingefasst. Es ermöglicht atemberaubende Ausblicke über die Weinfelder.

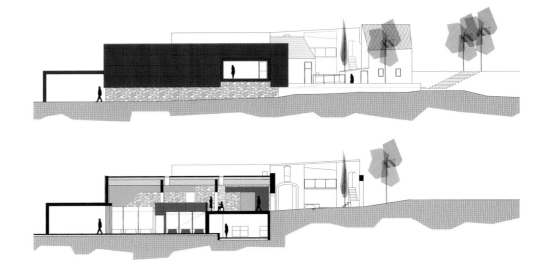

KELLEREI NALS-MARGREID
Nals, Italy

This project involved remodeling, extending and consolidating the production sites at this winery. The architectural solution included the construction of a new front building, intended for receiving deliveries, a grape storage facility with wine press, a large underground cellar and a barrique cellar. The production processes have also been rearranged and this reorganization permits views of the newly designed courtyard, wine press and barrique cellar. The front building has been constructed from red-brown concrete in response to the Porphyry rocks commonly found in the surrounding landscape. The folded roof is reminiscent of origami and this technique gives it optimal rigidity. The barrique cellar is reminiscent of an over-dimensional wine crate, located in the courtyard.

La tâche de l'architecte consistait à rénover un chai et à l'agrandir afin de réorganiser la production du vin. Le nouveau bâtiment, construit dans le prolongement de l'ancien, inclut une tour qui abrite le pressoir, ainsi qu'une cave de fermentation et un espace pour l'élevage du vin en barriques. La teinte terre de Sienne du béton utilisé pour cette extension s'harmonise parfaitement aux falaises en porphyre qui se dressent autour du vignoble. Le toit présente des plis façon origami qui en assurent la rigidité. Le volume qui abrite les barriques ressemble à une caisse de vin surdimensionnée. Ainsi réaménagé, ce chai permet de suivre les différentes étapes de la production, du pressage des grappes à l'élevage du vin.

Ziel des Projekts war, durch Umbau und die Erweiterung der bestehenden Gebäude die Produktionsabläufe zu optimieren. Erreicht wurde dies durch die Errichtung eines neuen Kopfgebäudes, das einen Kelterturm zur Anlieferung und Einkellerung der Trauben, einen großen unterirdischen Keller und einen Barriquekeller beherbergt. In Anlehnung an die umgebenden Porphyrfelsen wurde das neue Hauptgebäude in braunrötlichem Beton errichtet und fügt sich dadurch harmonisch in die umliegende Landschaft ein. Die Dachplatte wurde wie beim Origami gefaltet und so optimal ausgesteift; der Barriquekeller wurde wie eine überdimensionale Weinkiste als Holzbau in den Hof gestellt. So ergibt sich ein neu gestalteter Innenhof, der Einblicke in die Produktion im Kelterturm und dem Barriquekeller bietet.

Architect | Markus Scherer
Location | Heiligenberg 2, 39010 Nals, Italy
Year of completion | 2011
Client | Kellerei Nals-Margreid
Type of venue | winery
Type of wine | Pinot Blanc, Chardonnay, Pinot Gris,
Moscato Giallo, Müller-Thurgau, Kerner, Sauvignon,
Lagrein Rosé, Edelvernatsch, Grauvernatsch, Kal-
terersee Auslese, St. Magdalener, Pinot Noir, Lagrein,
Merlot, Cabernet
Number of seating places | 30
Cooling and ventilation techniques | convection
cooling
Trained sommelier | yes
Own vineyard | yes
Storage quality | ★★★★★

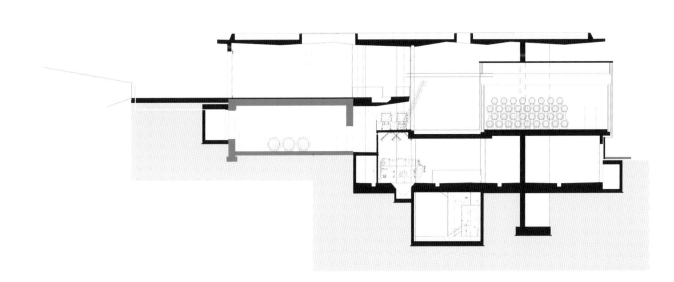

Architect | Planungsbüro Münzing
Lighting | Lichtpunkt Melanie Hübener
Location | Strümpfelbacher Straße 47, 70327 Stuttgart, Germany
Year of completion | 2012
Client | Weinmanufaktur Untertürkheim
Type of venue | retail
Type of wine | Trollinger, Riesling, Lemberger, Pinot Noir, Pinot Gris, Müller-Thurgau, Merlot
Number of seating places | 18
Own vineyard | yes
Storage quality | ★★★★☆

36

WEINMANUFAKTUR
UNTERTÜRKHEIM
Stuttgart, Germany

The new design of the sales area is characterized by a sensitive and complex handling of the materials and surfaces. The new heart of this wine producer – the storage space filled with oak barrels – is immediately visible through floor to ceiling windows when one enters the building, adjacent to the tasting area. Three shimmering gold sections divide the elongated sales area into four sections without spatially separating them from each other. Wine tasting islands – apparently dotted at random throughout the room – help create a relaxed impression, supported by the carefully orchestrated lighting design. The rooms combine old handicraft traditions with high-quality materials.

Un soin particulier a été apporté à la sélection des matériaux lors de la rénovation de ce magasin exclusivement dédié au vin. Les clients remarquent tout d'abord la « salle des barriques » entièrement vitrée, puis passent dans l'espace de dégustation à l'atmosphère feutrée. Vient ensuite une grande salle tout en longueur dans laquelle trois larges bandes dorées couvrant les murs et le plafond structurent l'espace sans le cloisonner. On y trouve des îlots de dégustation dont la disposition aléatoire s'allie à un éclairage sophistiqué pour générer une ambiance décontractée. Ce type de décoration intérieure joue sur deux tableaux : tradition artisanale et matériaux d'excellente qualité.

Ein sensibler und aufwändiger Umgang mit Material und Oberflächen ist das Leitmotiv für die Neugestaltung des Verkaufsraumes. Das neue Herz der Weinmanufaktur – das Barriquelager – wird bereits beim Eintreten durch eine raumhohe Verglasung in Szene gesetzt, ein ruhiger Degustationsraum schließt sich an. Drei gold-schimmernde Raumspangen teilen den langgestreckten Verkaufsraum in vier Abschnitte ohne ihn räumlich zu zerschneiden. Verkostungsinseln, wie zufällig im Raum verteilt, schaffen eine lockere Stimmung, unterstützt von einer vielseitigen, situationsbezogenen Beleuchtungsstrategie. Die Gestaltung der Räume verbindet alte Handwerkstraditionen mit hochwertigen Materialien.

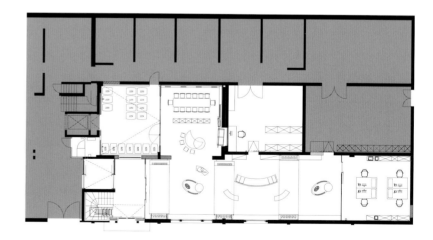

GUT HERMANNSBERG
Niederhausen-Nahe, Germany

In order to revitalize the Gut Hermannsberg complex, three existing buildings have been completely renovated and augmented by the addition of a new building. The new construction is positioned between the old historic wine pressing hall and the guesthouse, functioning as a connecting element joining the two. This part of the complex is clad with copper panels, a deliberate nod to the copper-colored foil used to seal the bottle tops, the etiquettes and emblem used on the company stationary. A garden and two balconies offering views over the vineyards, loungers, and a sun terrace are located above and adjacent to the bottle cellar. The historical wine pressing area has been transformed into offices, an indoor tasting area, additional guest rooms, a vinotheque and event space.

Dans le cadre de la revitalisation du domaine de Hermannsberg, jadis propriété du roi de Prusse, les architectes ont construit un nouveau bâtiment reliant l'ancienne maison de maître et le pressoir. Il s'agit d'un édifice pourvu d'une enveloppe en plaques de cuivre disposées comme des écailles, ce matériau (ou du moins sa couleur) se retrouvant sur le goulot des bouteilles, les étiquettes et le papier à en-tête du domaine. Le nouveau bâtiment se complète d'un jardin suspendu et de deux terrasses agrémentées de pergolas qui offrent des vues sur le vignoble. L'ancien pressoir abrite désormais des bureaux, un espace de dégustation, des chambres d'hôtes, une vinothèque et une salle événementielle.

Zur Revitalisierung der ehemaligen königlich-preußischen Weinbaudomäne Gut Hermannsberg wurden drei Bestandshäuser für Gäste umgebaut und durch einen Neubau ergänzt, der zwischen der alten historischen Kelterhalle und dem Gästehaus als neues Kelterhaus fungiert. Der Gebäudeteil wurde mit geschuppt verlegten Kupferplatten verkleidet, da Kupfer, beziehungsweise Kupferfarbe auch die Signaturfarbe für Flaschenverschlüsse, Etiketten und Geschäftspapier ist. Über und neben dem Flaschenkellerdach wurde ein Garten mit zwei Balkons für die Weinbergansicht angelegt sowie Liegeflächen und ein Sonnendeck. Die historische Kelterhalle wurde zu Büros, einem internen Verkostungsraum, Gästezimmern, Vinothek und Veranstaltungsraum umgenutzt.

Architect | Mahlau² Baukunst Drinnen & Draussen
Interior architect | Mahlau² Baukunst: Christiane
Mahlau, Bettina Hartmann
Location | Ehemalige Weinbaudomäne, 55585
Niederhausen-Nahe, Germany
Year of completion | 2013
Client | Dr. Christine Dinse and Jens Reidel
Type of venue | winery
Type of wine | Riesling
Number of seating places | 50
Own vineyard | yes
Storage quality | ★ ★ ★ ★ ★

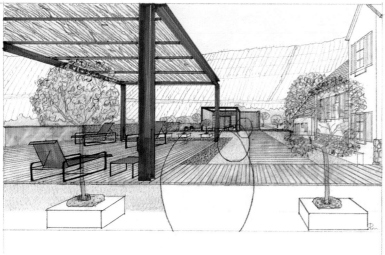

42

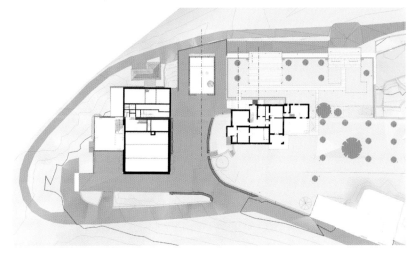

VINOTHEK MAX MÜLLER
Volkach, Germany

This winery, located within a historical complex from the 17th century, has been comprehensively refurbished; the partitions between the various rooms were removed in order to create space for sales, presentation and an additional office area. The new furnishings are arranged around the edge of the room and serve a number of different functions, acting simultaneously as seating elements, presentation objects and storage space. The key focus of the design is the new bar, which serves wine tasting, sales and administrative tasks. The glass partition subtly divides the office and sales areas. The pattern on the glass responds to the historical stucco ceiling found on the upper floors.

Le magasin de ce bâtiment classé datant du XVIIᵉ siècle a été entièrement rénové. Des cloisons y ont été supprimées de manière à le transformer en un vaste espace de vente et de dégustation se complétant par un bureau. L'architecte a positionné le long des murs des meubles intégrés tels que banquettes, présentoirs et placards. Le centre de la pièce est désormais occupé par un long plan de travail qui sert à la fois de comptoir et de bureau. Une vitre partiellement dépolie dont les motifs reproduisent des stucs toujours visibles aux étages supérieurs sépare le coin bureau de l'espace de vente et de dégustation.

In einem denkmalgeschützten Anwesen aus dem 17. Jahrhundert wurden die kleinteiligen Räume des bestehenden Weinverkaufs entkernt. So wurden Raumtrennungen entfernt, um einen großen Raum für Verkauf, Präsentation und Büronutzung zu schaffen. Die neuen Möbel entlang der Wände sind multifunktional konzipiert und dienen als Sitz-, Präsentations- und Staumöbel. Den Mittelpunkt des Raumes bildet die neue Theke, welche die Funktionen Verkosten, Verkaufen und Büroarbeit aufnimmt. Die Glasscheibe trennt subtil zwischen Büroarbeitsplatz und Weinverkauf und nimmt mit ihren Mustern Bezug auf die historische Stuckdecke in den Obergeschossen, deren markante Elemente abfotografiert und reduziert in das Glas geschliffen wurden.

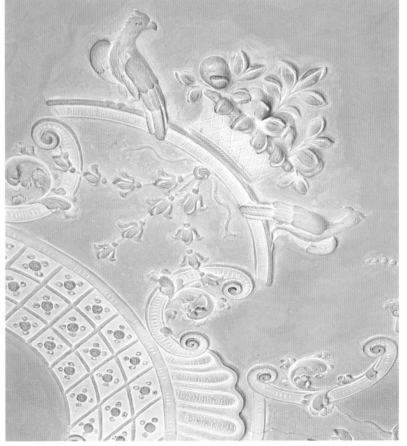

Architect | Architektur Büro Jäcklein
Location | Hauptstraße 46, 97332 Volkach, Germany
Year of completion | 2008
Client | Rainer and Monika Müller
Type of venue | retail
Type of wine | Silvaner, Riesling, Müller-Thurgau,
Pinot Blanc, Scheurebe, Pinot Noir, Domina
Number of seating places | 62
Trained sommelier | yes
Own vineyard | yes
Storage quality | ★★★☆☆

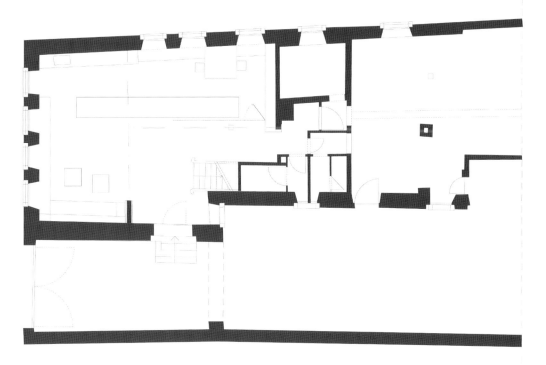

LES CAVES de TAILLEVENT

LES CAVES de TA

Architect | Pierre-Yves Rochon (PYR)
Location | 228, rue du Faubourg Saint-Honoré, 75008 Paris, France
Year of completion | 2012
Client | Groupe Taillevent
Type of venue | hospitality
Number of seating places | 70
Cooling and ventilation techniques | Provintech Machine
Trained sommelier | yes
Own vineyard | yes
Storage quality | ★★★★☆

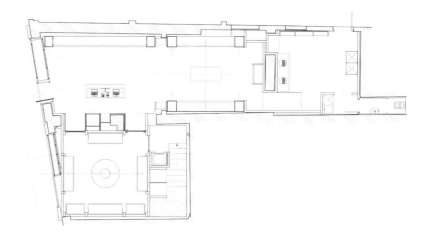

LES CAVES DE TAILLEVENT
Paris, France

This design concept developed by the Taillevent Group and PYR for Les 110 de Taillevent and Les Caves de Taillevent is all about making the French form of art-de-vivre accessible to a larger audience. The simple yet elegant interiors reflect nature, life and the art of wine growing. Honoring this theme, the dining room, tasting room, and retail areas are made of contoured oak, and the flooring runs horizontally across the veneer walls, reaching up to the ceiling. As a direct nod to wine casks, metal cask hoops circle the tabletops and are reimagined on the façade. The color palette is inspired by vineyards, with green velvet banquettes and rich earth tones, from the leather of the armchairs to the artwork on the walls.

En collaboration avec le groupe Taillevent, la société PYR a réaménagé Les Caves de Taillevent et la brasserie Les 100 de Taillevent afin de permettre à un plus large public d'apprécier l'art de vivre à la française. Le design retenu, simple mais élégant, rend hommage à la nature, à la vie et à la vigne. C'est pourquoi le sol, les murs et le plafond sont entièrement recouverts en bois de chêne dans le restaurant, la boutique et la salle de dégustation. Toujours dans le même ordre d'idées, des tables rondes ont été réalisées avec des cercles de barriques, tandis que le velours vert des banquettes ainsi que les riches tons terreux des fauteuils en cuir et des œuvres d'art accrochées aux murs renvoient à la palette de couleurs qui prévaut dans les vignobles.

Französisches Savoir-Vivre einem breiterem Publikum zugänglich zu machen, war der Ausgangspunkt für das von der Groupe Taillevent und PYR entwickelte Designkonzept für Les 110 de Taillevent und Les Caves de Taillevent. Die einfach gehaltene Innenarchitektur stellt einen Bezug zur Natur, dem Leben und der Kunst der Weinherstellung her. Der Verkaufsbereich sowie der Speise- und Verkostungsraum wurden mit rauem Eichenholz verkleidet, welches an den Wänden horizontal als Furnier verläuft und bis zur Decke reicht. Als Reminiszenz an die Weinherstellung wurden die Tischplatten mit metallenen Fassreifen umspannt. Auch die Farbgestaltung – von den Sesseln bis hin zu den Kunstwerken – orientiert sich mit grünen und erdfarbenen Tönen an den natürlichen Farben der Weinberge.

GRAHAM'S 1890 LODGE
Vila Nova de Gaia, Portugal

Architect | Luís Loureiro Arquitecto
Designers | P-06 Atelier-Nuno Gusmão, Giuseppe Greco, Joana Proserpio
Location | Rua do Agro 141, 4400-281 Vila Nova de Gaia, Portugal
Year of completion | 2013
Client | W. & J. Graham's
Type of venue | hospitality
Type of wine | port, red and white wine
Number of seating places | 250
Trained sommelier | yes
Own vineyard | yes
Storage quality | ★ ★ ★ ☆ ☆

The Graham's Lodge was built in 1890, and has been open to visitors since 1993, and features a tasting area where visitors can enjoy port, and an adjacent shop and wine bar. Upon arriving at the lodge, visitors are given a guided tour of the facilities and the 3,200 casks of maturing port. The guided tour also includes the dark vintage wine cellar, where Graham's vintage ports are kept. In early 2011 the Symington family decided to invest in the renovation of the lodge, not just to accommodate the ever increasing numbers of visitors, but also to provide them with a much more interesting experience during their visit. At the end of the visit costumers are invited to enjoy a light meal in the new wine bar, or better still, in the new Vinum restaurant.

La cave à porto Graham's Lodge date de 1890 et est ouverte au public depuis 1993. On y trouve une salle de dégustation, une boutique et un bar. La visite guidée permet notamment de découvrir les 3200 tonneaux dans lesquels le porto s'affine, ainsi que la salle vintage où l'on peut goûter le meilleur du porto Graham's. L'établissement, repris par la famille Symington en 2011, a entre-temps été rénové et agrandi afin de répondre au nombre croissant de visiteurs. Au terme de la visite, les amateurs de porto peuvent prendre une collation au bar ou — encore mieux — s'attabler au tout nouveau restaurant Vinum.

Im Jahre 1993 wurde die Graham's Lodge für Besucher geöffnet und verfügt seitdem über einen Verkostungsbereich zur Probe der Portweine, einen angeschlossenen Laden und eine Weinbar. Bei ihrer Ankunft auf dem Gelände werden Besucher zu einer Besichtigung der 3.200 Fässer reifenden Portweins eingeladen. Die Tour beinhaltet auch einen Besuch der alten Weinkeller, in denen Graham's Portwein gelagert wird. 2011 beschloss die Symington Familie die Lodge renovieren zu lassen, nicht nur um die steigende Anzahl an Gästen unterbringen zu können, sondern auch um das Erlebnis des Aufenthalts zu verbessern. Der Abschluss einer jeden Tour bildet ein Besuch der Weinbar oder des Vinum Restaurants, in denen die Besucher leichte Kost aus der hauseigenen Küche probieren können.

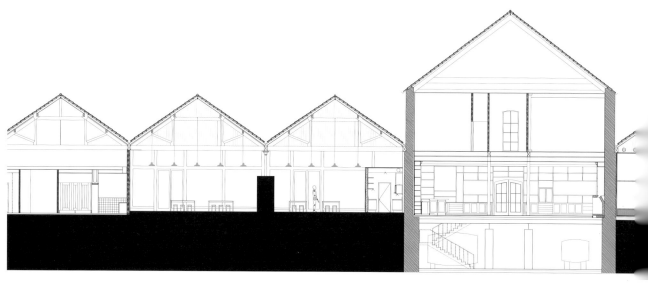

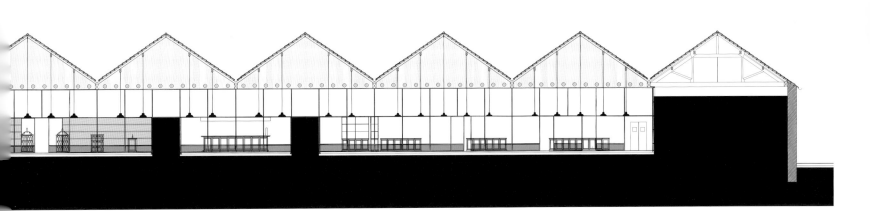

Architect | Architekturbüro Mertens
Location | Rotweinstraße 7–9, 53506 Rech/Ahr, Germany
Year of completion | 2007
Client | Stodden family
Type of venue | winery
Type of wine | Pinot Noir Précoce, Pinot Noir, Riesling
Number of seating places | 40
Own vineyard | yes
Storage quality | ★★★☆☆

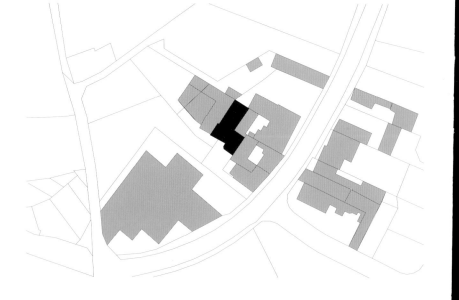

ROTWEINGUT JEAN STODDEN
Rech/Ahr, Germany

Rethinking wine also requires a rethinking of architecture itself. The task facing the architects was to formulate this train of thought architecturally. The main materials used for the interior design comprise oak used in the wine cellar and sandstone taken from the vineyards. The unusual use of these two materials gives the interior a unique appearance and affords a new perspective. Oak parquet has been used on the walls in both the sales area and in the tasting room. The stones used for the supporting walls have also been used to make the large flooring tiles. The careful attention to detail creates a space with soul that is in keeping with the high quality of the products and the architecture.

Une nouvelle approche du vin requiert une nouvelle approche du design. C'est pourquoi l'architecte a conçu la décoration intérieure en privilégiant deux matériaux inhabituels susceptibles de renouveler la manière dont les clients perçoivent l'espace : le bois de chêne et le grauwacke qu'on trouve sur les coteaux environnants. Le chêne a été utilisé comme revêtement mural dans la boutique et la grande salle de dégustation, tandis que le grauwacke se retrouve à la fois dans les murs en gabions et sous forme de grandes dalles. L'amour du détail a ainsi permis de créer un espace doté d'une âme — Un espace pour les amoureux du vin, d'une qualité architecturale n'ayant d'égale que l'excellence des crus proposés à la vente.

Wer Wein neu denkt, denkt folgerichtig auch Architektur neu. Die Architekten überführten diesen Gedanken in eine bauliche Struktur. Die Eiche des Weinkellers und die Grauwacke an den Hängen des Weinberges sind die wesentlichen Materialien des Innenausbaus. Die ungewöhnliche Anwendung dieser beiden Materialien fördert ein neues Sehen und eine neue Wahrnehmung. Das Eichenparkett wurde sowohl im Verkaufsraum als auch im großen Probiersaal an die Wände gebracht. Die Grauwacke der Stützmauern kommt traditionell als Bodenbelag in großen Abmessungen zur Anwendung. Bis ins Detail entstanden Räume mit Seele, die dem sinnlichen Weingenuss eine Plattform geben und der hohen Qualität des Produktes eine entsprechend qualitätsvolle Architektur entgegenstellen.

PINOTECA POSS
Windesheim, Germany

The reduced building envelope with light-flooded filigree glass elements provides the perfect canvas for the realization of the architects' design ideas. The spatial concept is characterized by the synonymy of the materials and the wine. With its reduced wooden cubic form built from local wood, the 'floating' reception desk is a focal point of the design. The acoustic suspended ceiling above the desk is illuminated with both direct and indirect lighting, which helps to subtly draw it into focus. The wine draws its flavor from the slate soil, and this is represented by the use of slate in the interior design. The cement flooring gives the wine tasting area a warm atmosphere. The stylish design expresses the quality of the product and the high standards adhered to by the winegrowers.

Ce bâtiment a été conçu selon deux principes directeurs : enveloppe minimaliste en verre optimisant l'éclairage naturel et utilisation de matériaux en rapport avec le vin. L'intérieur est dominé par un comptoir en bois d'origine locale, long parallélépipède semblant suspendu dans l'air et éclairé par des spots et des dispositifs d'éclairage indirect intégrés au faux plafond contribuant à une meilleure acoustique. On remarque également une niche aménagée dans une cloison recouverte d'ardoise — autre matériau d'origine locale —, tandis que le sol en ciment couleur sable qui renvoie à la terre du vignoble génère une atmosphère chaleureuse. La qualité architecturale s'affirme ainsi comme le pendant de l'excellence du cru.

Der Entwurf basiert auf einer reduzierten, lichtdurchfluteten Gebäudehülle aus filigranen Glaselementen sowie der Verwendung von Materialien, die einen Bezug zu den angebauten Weinen herstellen. Das Herzstück ist die kubistische, schwebende Theke, welche komplett aus heimischem Holz gefertigt wurde. Zusammen mit dem darüberliegenden akustischen Deckensegel und dessen direkter und indirekter Beleuchtung bildet sie den Mittelpunkt des Raumes. Die aus Schieferplatten bestehende Nische und Trennwand verweist auf den Schieferboden, während der farblich an Sand erinnernde Zementboden einen Bezug zum Anbaugrund herstellt und gleichzeitig eine warme Atmosphäre schafft. So wurde ein Gebäude kreiert, welches den Anspruch der Winzer an ihr Produkt eindrucksvoll interpretiert.

Architect | planungsbüro i21-Heiko Gruber
Location | Goldgrube 20–22, 55452 Windesheim,
Germany
Year of completion | 2011
Client | Weingut Poss
Type of venue | winery
Type of wine | Burgundy
Number of seating places | 8–20
Own vineyard | yes
Storage quality | ★★★★☆

64

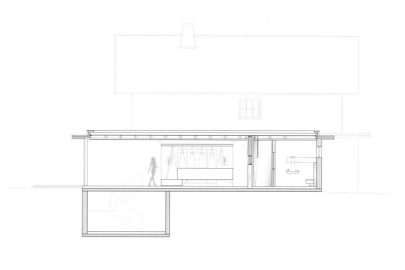

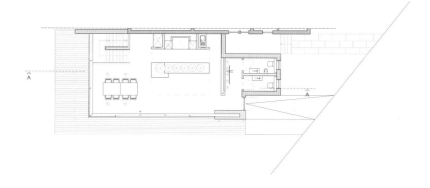

RED PIF WINE SHOP AND RESTAURANT
Prague, Czech Republic

This interior design is characterized by the high-quality craftsmanship of the materials used, including the use of oak wood for the floor, bar and shelves. The remodeling work brings the original character of the 19th-century building to the fore, reestablishing an authentic quality. The existing shop windows establish contact with the outside world, an extremely important feature for a city restaurant. The architects also designed the rotating screens that serve evening wine tasting sessions or private parties. Large wine bottle shapes have been cut out of the shelving units and transformed into a design feature in their own right.

La décoration intérieure, caractérisée par la qualité des matériaux choisis — notamment le chêne utilisé pour le parquet, le bar et les étagères — ainsi que par le soin avec lequel ils ont été travaillés, est le résultat d'une rénovation visant à rendre au bâtiment l'aspect qu'il avait lors de sa construction au XIXe siècle. Les fenêtres qui ouvrent la boutique sur la rue sont pourvues de volets que l'architecte a conçus en forme de bouteilles. Lorsqu'ils sont fermés, ces volets permettent de créer une atmosphère plus intime, par exemple lors d'une soirée de dégustation.

Das Interieur wird von hochwertigen, nach handwerklicher Tradition verarbeiteten Materialien charakterisiert. So wurden zum Beispiel der Boden, die Bar und die Regale komplett aus Eichenholz gefertigt. Die Umgestaltung hat den ursprünglichen Charakter des Gebäudes aus dem 19. Jahrhundert wiederhergestellt. Die vorhandenen Fenster schaffen die für ein Stadtrestaurant wichtige Verbindung zur Außenwelt und können durch die ebenfalls von den Architekten entworfenen, als Weinflaschen geformten, Fensterläden verschlossen werden, so dass ein privater Raum für Weinproben oder geschlossene Veranstaltungen entsteht.

Architect | Aulík Fišer architekti – Jakub Fišer, Petra Skalická
Location | U Dobřenských 1, Prague 1, Czech Republic
Year of completion | 2010
Client | K4wines
Type of venue | hospitality
Type of wine | natural French wines, Czech wines
Number of seating places | 46
Cooling and ventilation techniques | fan-coils
Trained sommelier | yes
Storage quality | ★★★☆☆

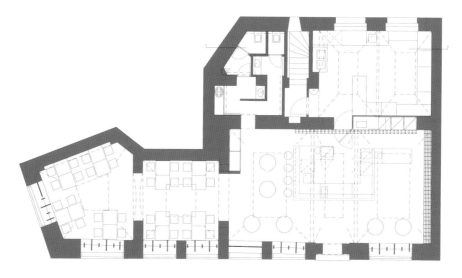

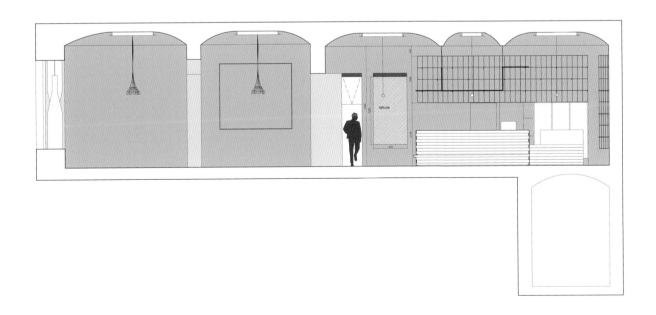

Architect | Raëd Abillama Architects
Location | Basbina, Batroun, Lebanon
Year of completion | 2012
Client | IXSIR Winery
Type of venue | winery
Type of wine | red, white and rosé, dry wines, blended wines
Number of seating places | 80 inside, 120 outside, 30 in the tasting room
Cooling and ventilation techniques | natural cooling and minimal air conditioning, mechanical
ventilation for CO_2 extraction
Trained sommelier | yes
Own vineyard | yes
Storage quality | ★★★★★

70

IXSIR WINERY
Batroun, Lebanon

Embedded into the lush green landscape on the outskirts of Basbina, this winery and vineyard overlook the coast and surrounding areas. The design focused on establishing a dialogue between the built and natural environments. The main building houses the reception area and is the focal point of the entire ensemble. A staircase leads from the reception area underground to the cellar, vats, storage racks, and operational areas. The entire design is designed to perfectly fit the topography of the sloping site, and the winemaking process unravels as one follows the sloping ramp downwards through the individual areas. The wine cellars are completely submerged below ground, creating the desired equilibrium of temperature and humidity.

Ce chai et son vignoble dominent la ville de Bazbina, ses environs verdoyants et la mer qu'on aperçoit à l'horizon. L'architecte s'est efforcé d'établir un dialogue entre le bâti et son environnement naturel. Dans le bâtiment central de ce complexe parfaitement adapté à la topographie d'un terrain en pente, un escalier part de la réception pour desservir la cave où se trouve une rampe qui mène aux espaces techniques souterrains et offre un aperçu des différentes étapes de la vinification. Le vin est exclusivement stocké sous terre de manière à lui faire profiter des meilleures conditions de température et d'hygrométrie.

Eingebettet in die üppige grüne Landschaft um Basbina bietet dieses Weingut einen spektakulären Ausblick über die Küste und die umliegenden Gegenden. Die Beziehung zur natürlichen Umwelt stand im Zentrum des Entwurfs. Das Hauptgebäude, welches den Schwerpunkt des Ensembles bildet, beherbergt den Empfangsbereich und den Zugang zu den unterirdischen Einrichtungen – dem Weinkeller und den verschiedenen Produktionsstätten. Der gesamte Entwurf passt sich perfekt in die Topographie des Geländes ein. Zentrales Element ist die abschüssige Rampe, die auf dem Weg nach unten Einblicke in die einzelnen Schritte der Weinproduktion ermöglicht. Sie mündet im komplett unterirdischen Weinkeller, der die für den Lagerprozess notwendige Balance zwischen Temperatur und Feuchtigkeit bietet.

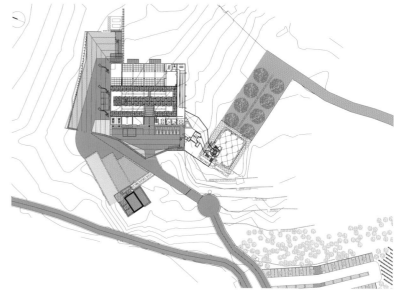

LE MONDE WINE TASTING ROOM
Prata di Pordenone, Italy

Architect | Alessandro Isola
Location | Via Garibaldi 2, Loc. Le Monde, 38080 Prata di Pordenone, Italy
Year of completion | 2014
Client | Società Agricola Le Monde
Type of venue | winery
Type of wine | Prosecco, Pinot Bianco, Ribolla Gialla, Pinot Grigio, Friulano, Chardonnay, Sauvignon, Inaco Riserva 2008, Refosco dal Penduncolo Rosso, Cabernet Franc, Cabernet Sauvignon
Number of seating places | 44
Cooling and ventilation techniques | ventilation duct, exposed pipes below trusses bring in air; exhaust air drawn through floor grills
Trained sommelier | yes
Own vineyard | yes
Storage quality | ★ ★ ★ ☆ ☆

The focus of this wine tasting room project was to create a space devoted to sensory experience that ensured a constant visual connection with the surrounding vineyards. The award winning Le Monde winery nestles between the sea and the hills of north-east Italy, an area steeped in traditional wine culture. To enhance this connection, two large tasting tables extend in line with the rows of vines that stretch as far as the eye can see. The wine fridges and bottle display are located at the front of the room. The main counter sits in front of the wall display and functions as both kitchen and feature bottle display. The overall result is a room that is at one with its surroundings and offers visitors a beautiful environment where they can sample the award winning produce of this fine Italian winery.

Le chai Le Monde fait partie d'un vignoble multiséculaire situé dans les collines du nord-est de l'Italie à proximité de la mer. La tâche des architectes consistait ici à créer une salle de dégustation en contact visuel avec les vignes. Ce contact est assuré par deux longues tables en bois massif positionnées dans l'alignement des rangs de vigne semblant s'étendre jusqu'à l'horizon. Du côté du pignon largement vitré se trouvent les étagères à bouteilles et les caves à vin réfrigérées, ainsi qu'un comptoir qui sert aussi de coin cuisine et de présentoir. Le bâtiment dans son ensemble forme un espace en harmonie avec son environnement, dans lequel les visiteurs peuvent savourer à leur aise un cru plusieurs fois primé.

Das international ausgezeichnete Weingut Le Monde liegt im Nordosten Italiens, in einem der traditionsreichsten Weinanbaugebiete des Landes. Um diese lokale Verbundenheit zu verdeutlichen wurde ein Verkostungsraum geschaffen, der durch seinen Charakter sinnliches Erleben steigert und eine visuelle Beziehung zu den um-liegenden Weinfeldern schafft. Zwei große Tische erstrecken sich parallel zu den Weinreben außerhalb des Gebäudes, die bis an den Horizont zu reichen scheinen. Die Weinschränke und Präsentationsregale wurden an der Stirnseite des Raumes platziert. Davor befindet sich die Haupttheke, welche sowohl als Küche als auch zur Präsentation des aktuellen Weines dient. Im Gesamtbild ergibt sich so ein Raum, der konsequent die Landschaft in sein Inneres führt und ein perfektes Ambiente zur Probe der preisgekrönten Weine bietet.

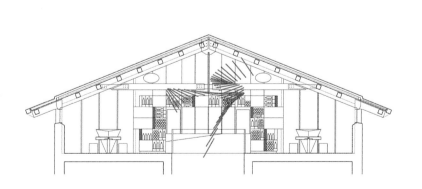

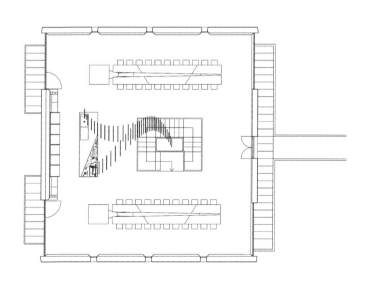

Architect | Promontorio
Interior design | StudioMK27, Promontorio
Location | 7050 Montemor-o-Novo, Portugal
Year of completion | 2011
Client | Sousa Cunhal Tourism SGPS
Type of venue | hospitality
Type of wine | Touriga Nacional, Alicante Bouschet, Touriga Franca
Number of seating places | 160
Trained sommelier | yes
Own vineyard | yes

L'AND VINEYARDS HOTEL
Montemor-o-Novo, Portugal

Integrated in the L'And Vineyards resort, this design involved a new building for a family-based wine making and agricultural company. The hotel is the key focus of the entire ensemble, housing the reception, clubhouse, restaurant, spa with indoor pool, and the service support to the adjacent suites. In addition, the building also functions as a winery, where guests can experience the whole wine making process, from grape selection, crushing, fermentation and pressing, to barrel aging, blending, filtering and bottling. The building was conceived as a hinged prism with four corners removed to create areas of shade and intimacy.

Le projet consistait ici à construire un hôtel devant compléter une exploitation viticole familiale. Le nouveau bâtiment abrite la réception, les suites, le club, le restaurant et l'espace bien-être avec piscine couverte, ainsi que différents locaux techniques. Les clients de cet hôtel insolite doublé d'un chai peuvent suivre toutes les étapes du processus de vinification : sélection des grappes, pressage, fermentation, élevage du vin en fûts, filtrage et mise en bouteilles. La forme prismatique du bâtiment tient à ce que les quatre coins supérieurs du parallélépipède ont été tronqués de manière à créer des espaces à la fois lumineux et à l'abri des regards.

Dieser Entwurf beinhaltet ein neues Gebäude für ein familiengeführtes Weingut und Landwirtschaftsunternehmen auf dem Gelände des L'And Wein-Resorts. Das Hotel bildet das Zentrum des gesamten Ensembles und beherbergt die Rezeption, das Clubhaus, ein Restaurant, ein Spa mit Indoorpool und Servicebereiche für die benachbarten Suiten. Zudem dient es als Weinkellerei, in der die Gäste den gesamten Prozess der Weinherstellung von der Auswahl und dem Pressen der Trauben über die Lagerung und den Ausbau bis hin zur Filtration und Abfüllung erleben können. Die Gebäudeform erinnert an ein aufgeklapptes Prisma, dessen Ecken entfernt wurden, um schattige und geschützte Räume zu erzeugen.

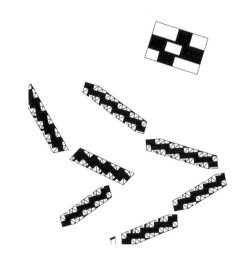

Architect | Fabrika
Structural engineers | Produkcija 004
Location | Vale 78, 52470 Buje, Croatia
Year of completion | 2012
Client | Kozlović Winery
Type of venue | winery
Type of wine | indigenous Istrian varieties
Number of seating places | 20
Cooling and ventilation techniques | Mitsubishi VRF (Variable Refrigerant Flow) system
Trained sommelier | yes
Own vineyard | yes
Storage quality | ★★★☆☆

KOZLOVIĆ WINERY
Buje, Croatia

The Kozlović Winery is located on the Istrian peninsula in Croatia, 12 kilometers from the Adriatic coast. The Kozlović family has been producing wines for four generations and this is one of the most internationally renowned Croatian wineries. The clean-cut rectangular building rises up from the middle of the vineyards, and is yet almost invisible thanks to its carefully designed façade. The façade design makes striking use of aluminum plates designed to look like the branches of grapevines, while the flat roof is planted with lavender bushes and flowers. The winery boasts a large tasting room for wine tasting and corporate meetings, as well as customized wine events. A bar and summer terrace stretch above the vineyards.

Ce vignoble est situé en Croatie, dans la péninsule d'Istrie, à une douzaine de kilomètres de la côte adriatique. Depuis quatre générations, la famille Kozlović produit un vin reconnu dans le monde entier comme l'un des meilleurs du pays. Le nouveau bâtiment, de plan rectangulaire et aux lignes clairement définies, surplombe le vignoble et s'y intègre parfaitement grâce aux plaques d'aluminium de la façade découpées en forme de ceps stylisés, grâce également au toit sur lequel poussent des fleurs et des plants de lavande. On trouve à l'intérieur une vaste salle de dégustation qui peut être utilisée pour des événements en rapport avec le vin. L'ensemble se complète par un bar avec terrasse dominant les vignes.

Das Weingut Kozlović liegt auf der Halbinsel Istrien, zwölf Kilometer von der Küste des Mittelmeeres entfernt. Es wird von der Familie Kozlović in der vierten Generation bewirtschaftet und gehört zu den bekanntesten Weinproduzenten Kroatiens. Das streng definierte, auf einem rechtwinkligen Grundriss basierende Hauptgebäude erhebt sich inmitten der Weinberge und ist dank seiner kunstvoll gestalteten Fassade dennoch fast unsichtbar. Die Verkleidung aus speziell gefertigten Aluminiumplatten imitiert die Zweige der Weinreben, während das bepflanzte Flachdach mit Lavendelbüschen und lokalen Pflanzen mit der Umgebung verschmilzt. Im Inneren beherbergt das Gebäude einen großen Raum für Weinproben und Veranstaltungen, während eine Bar und eine Terrasse weite Ausblicke über die Reben ermöglichen.

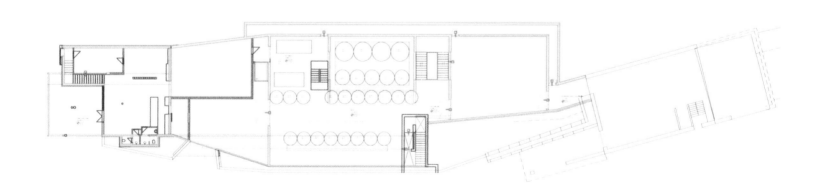

Architect | atelier-f architekten
Location | Porta Raetia, 7306 Fläsch, Switzerland
Year of completion | 2014
Client | Andrea Davaz family
Type of venue | winery
Type of wine | Pinot noir, Riesling, Silvaner, Chardonnay, Pinot gris, Pinot blanc, Sauvignon blanc, La Sara, Schiller
Number of seating places | 80
Cooling and ventilation techniques | heat pump
Trained sommelier | yes
Own vineyard | yes
Storage quality | ★★★★★

92

WEINGUT DAVAZ
Fläsch, Switzerland

This winery frames a large courtyard and working area. Although the ensemble has been created piece by piece, it nevertheless appears as a unified whole. Just a few main materials have been meticulously selected and implemented with careful attention to detail. In the barrel cellar, the ceiling is made of arched iron plates, while the walls have been built of rammed concrete. The exterior appearance of the cubic volume is characterized by a shallow saddle roof, window openings with concrete frames and rough plaster. The courtyard garden in front of the tasting area on the upper floor features herb beds and pergolas. The winery enjoys fantastic views of the vineyards.

Les bâtiments de ce domaine viticole, regroupés autour d'une grande cour, forment un ensemble bien qu'ils aient été construits à des époques différentes. Cela tient principalement au fait qu'ils n'intègrent qu'une gamme de matériaux restreinte, qui plus est travaillés avec soin. Ainsi, la cave où sont entreposées les barriques est dotée de murs en béton coulé et d'un plafond en plaques d'acier Corten légèrement voûtées, tandis que le bâtiment construit au-dessus, couvert d'un toit à deux faibles pentes, présente des murs recouverts d'un enduit grossier percés de fenêtres judicieusement positionnées dont l'encadrement est lui aussi en béton. La salle de dégustation donne sur un jardin avec pergola planté d'herbes aromatiques d'où l'on peut apprécier un superbe panorama sur les montagnes environnantes.

Das Weingut rahmt einen großen Hof und Arbeitsbereich ein. Obwohl es Stück für Stück entstand, erscheint es als geschlossenes Ensemble. Für den Bau wurden nur wenige, sorgfältig ausgewählte Materialien verwendet und mit einem Blick für das Detail verarbeitet. So verfügt der Barriquekeller über eine Decke aus oxidierten, gewölbten Eisenplatten und Wänden aus Schüttbeton, während die äußere Erscheinung der kubischen Baukörper von flachgeneigten Satteldächern, sorgfältig gesetzten Fensteröffnungen mit Betonrahmen und grobem Wandputz geprägt wird. Der Hofgarten vor dem Degustationsraum im Obergeschoss wurde mit Kräuterbeeten und einer Pergola gestaltet. Von dort eröffnet sich eine überwältigende Sicht in die Weinberge.

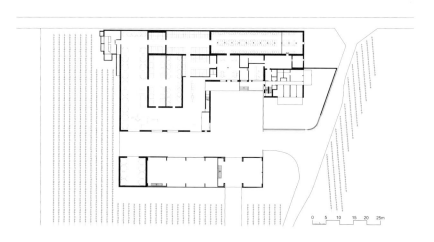

LA CABUCHE
Dardagny, Switzerland

The location of this project is characterized by an immediate sense of calm and tranquility. The stone building rises out of the surrounding vineyards to welcome Sunday strollers, passersby and anyone who wishes to relax over a glass of wine or enjoy a light meal. A covered terrace also gives guests the opportunity to enjoy sweeping views of the surrounding countryside, with the twinkling city lights visible in the distance during the evening. The interior is modern and welcoming, with bright colors and bright lighting contrasting the solid wood furnishings.

Cette maison en pierre de type traditionnel est située au calme au milieu des vignes. Elle abrite un restaurant qui constitue une halte appréciée des randonneurs, des promeneurs et de toute personne souhaitant savourer du bon vin et prendre une collation. Une terrasse couverte par une structure ultra-légère permet d'apprécier un panorama qui englobe une ville dont on aperçoit les lumières au loin au crépuscule. La décoration intérieure se caractérise par des teintes neutres et un éclairage au néon dont la modernité contraste avec des meubles traditionnels en bois massif.

Inmitten der Ruhe und Zurückgezogenheit der umliegenden Weinfelder gelegen, heißt dieses in traditioneller Steinbauweise errichtete Gebäude Tagesausflügler, Wanderer und jeden willkommen, der bei einem Glas Wein und leichter Küche entspannen möchte. Die mit einer kaum sichtbaren Aufhängung überdachte Terrasse bietet den Gästen weite Ausblicke über die umliegende Landschaft, in welcher die Lichter der Stadt bei Dämmerung am Horizont aufblitzen. Im modernen Interieur kontrastieren helle Farben und strahlende Beleuchtung mit den Einbauten aus Massivholz.

Architect | Bureau A
Location | 1283 Dardagny, Switzerland
Year of completion | 2013
Client | La Cabuche
Type of venue | hospitality
Type of wine | Gamay, Vin Blanc
Number of seating places | 20

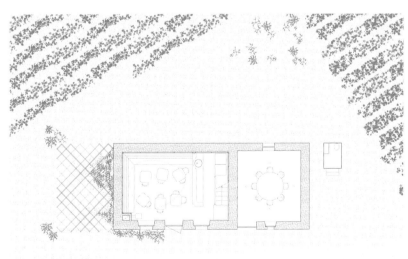

AFFENTALER WINZER-GENOSSENSCHAFT
Bühl, Germany

Originally built in 1980, this vineyard complex belongs to a winegrowers' cooperative in Affental, Germany. Comprehensive renovation work was carried out in two building phases and included completely reorganizing the ground floor, which houses the entrance, tasting area, sales area, foyer and a small hall with kitchen. The cellar accommodates a large room that can be subdivided into smaller areas if necessary and a new access system makes it accessible from both sides. A new kitchen meets commercial requirements. All technological installations and fire prevention mechanisms have also been renewed.

Les bâtiments de la coopérative agricole d'Affental, construits en 1980, ont été rénovés en deux étapes. Le rez-de-chaussée abritant l'entrée, l'espace de dégustation/vente, le foyer et la petite salle de réunion avec cuisine a été entièrement réorganisé. Quant à la grande salle du sous-sol, elle dispose désormais d'une cuisine aux normes et est divisible en deux moitiés pourvues d'une entrée séparée de sorte qu'elle peut être utilisée de manière plus intensive. De plus, dans le cadre de la rénovation, le système de protection contre l'incendie ainsi que tous les équipements techniques ont été modernisés.

Die umfassende Renovierung des Gebäudes der Affentaler Winzergenossenschaft aus dem Jahr 1980 wurde in zwei Bauabschnitten durchgeführt. Das Erdgeschoss mit den Bereichen Entrée, Weinverkostung, Weinverkauf, Foyer und kleiner Saal mit Küche erhielt eine komplett neue Raumorganisation. Das Untergeschoss wurde für eine intensivere Nutzung umgestaltet, indem der große Saal eine neue unabhängige Erschließung der zwei trennbaren Hälften und eine Küche erhielt, die gewerblichen Anforderungen entspricht. Zudem wurden die gesamte Haustechnik und der Brandschutz modernisiert.

Architect | Andreas Weber Architektur + Design
Interior architect | Andreas Weber Architektur +
Design, Barbara Adelmann-Weber
Location | Betschgräbler Platz, 77815 Bühl, Germany
Year of completion | 2013
Client | Affentaler Winzergenossenschaft Bühl
Type of venue | retail
Type of wine | Riesling, Traminer, Pinot Gris, Pinot
Blanc, Rivaner, Vin Gris, Pinot Noir red and rosé
Number of seating places | 150
Trained sommelier | yes
Own vineyard | yes
Storage quality | ★★★☆☆

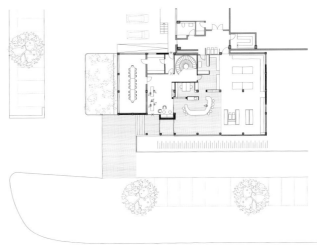

CEHEGIN WINE SCHOOL
Cehegín, Spain

Located in a traditional winemaking region in Spain, this project involved the transformation of a 17th-century wine cellar into a new cultural space. The cellar is characterized by its unique atmosphere, with its roughly hewn stonewalls and uneven arches. The design respects the original workmanship, leaving its character intact but breathing new life into the space. The old wine vats have been preserved by covering them with a large glass panel. The front part of the cellar now serves as a wine shop, with large shelving units displaying a variety of products. The project was financed by the European Agricultural Fund for Rural Development, Comunidad Autónoma de la Región de Murcia and Cehegín City Hall.

Ce chai construit au XVIIᵉ siècle dans une région d'Andalousie de longue tradition viticole a été récemment réaménagé pour en faire un espace événementiel. Les architectes se sont efforcés de conserver l'aspect d'origine, caractérisé par des voûtes et des murs irréguliers taillés dans le roc, tout en insufflant une nouvelle vie à ce lieu d'exception. Les grandes jarres autrefois utilisées pour la vinification sont restées sur place et sont désormais visibles sous un sol en verre. De plus, une salle de dégustation/vente pourvue d'étagères s'élevant sur toute la hauteur du mur a été aménagée dans la cave. Le projet a été financé par le Fonds européen agricole pour le développement rural, la communauté autonome de Murcie et la municipalité de Cehegín.

Ein Weinkeller aus dem 17. Jahrhundert wurde hier in einen neuen Veranstaltungsraum umgewandelt. In einer der traditionellen Weinanbauregionen Spaniens gelegen, verfügt der Keller durch seine roh behauenen Steinwände und ungleichmäßigen Gewölbebögen über eine einmalige Atmosphäre. Ziel der Umgestaltung war es, den Originalcharakter zu erhalten und gleichzeitig dem Bauwerk neues Leben einzuhauchen. Die alten Weingefäße wurden erhalten und mit einem gläsernen Fußboden überspannt. Im vorderen Bereich des Kellers wurde ein Weinladen mit großen Regaleinheiten eingerichtet. Das Projekt wurde durch den Europäischen Landwirtschaftsfonds für die Entwicklung des ländlichen Raums, die autonome Region Murcia und die Stadt Cehegín finanziert.

Architect | Inmat Arquitectura / Jose Luis Lopez Ibañez
Wine specialist | Pedro Martinez Fernandez
Location | Calle Pérez Villanueva 51, Casa de la Tercia,
30430 Cehegín, Spain
Year of completion | 2014
Client | Cehegín City Hall
Type of venue | culture
Number of seating places | 20
Storage quality | ★★★☆☆

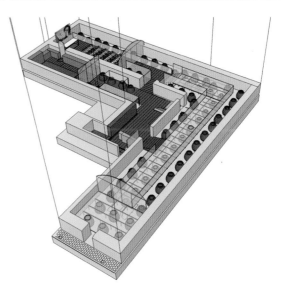

MERUS WINERY
St. Helena, CA, USA

Architect | Uxus
Location | 424 Crystal Springs Rd, St. Helena, CA 94574, USA
Year of completion | 2009
Client | Merus
Type of venue | winery
Type of wine | Cabernet Sauvignon
Number of seating places | approx. 45
Cooling and ventilation techniques | manual temperature control
Trained sommelier | yes
Own vineyard | yes
Storage quality | ★ ★ ★ ★ ★

Merus has been transformed from a premium artisanal cult wine to a true luxury product of the highest level. Uxus was commissioned to create an experience where customers are enveloped in the excellence and complexity of the brand. The objective was to create a winery that embodies all the Merus brand values of undiluted sophistication, complexity and quality. The winery's interior concept is refined heritage with modern sophistication and monotone classic furnishings with a contemporary twist. Mixed styles and periods come together to create an exciting and unforgettable atmosphere. Real objects, such as wine barrels and wine crates, create surprising compositions that exude information about their past use, giving a sense of history and soul to the spaces.

Le Merus, vin artisanal à l'origine, est devenu un produit de luxe en l'espace de deux décennies. Afin de répondre à ce succès, le bureau d'architectes Uxus a été chargé de rénover les locaux de manière à ce que les consommateurs puissent s'immerger dans l'excellence de la marque. Le nouveau design se devait de refléter les valeurs typiques du cru : qualité, raffinement et complexité. C'est pourquoi les architectes ont opté pour un savant dosage entre respect du patrimoine, amour du détail et clins d'œil à la modernité. Ce mélange des styles et des époques génère une atmosphère inoubliable, les barriques et caisses de bouteilles de jadis formant des compositions qui racontent une histoire du passé tout en donnant une âme aux différents espaces.

Die Weine von Merus entwickelten sich von einem exzellenten Geheimtipp zu einem wahren Luxusprodukt der höchsten Qualitätsstufe. Uxus wurde damit beauftragt eine Architektur zu schaffen, welche den Kunden die Exklusivität und Komplexität der Weine erleben lässt und für den hohen Anspruch der Marke steht: Qualität, Perfektion und Vielschichtigkeit. Das Konzept der Innenarchitektur orientiert sich an ausgewählten traditionellen Elementen, gemischt mit raffinierten, modernen Akzenten und zeitgenössisch anmutenden Möbelklassikern. Unterschiedliche Stile und Epochen verschmelzen zu einer einzigartigen, spannenden Atmosphäre, in der Objekte wie gebrauchte Weinfässer und -kisten einen Bezug zur Vergangenheit und zur Geschichte des Ortes herstellen.

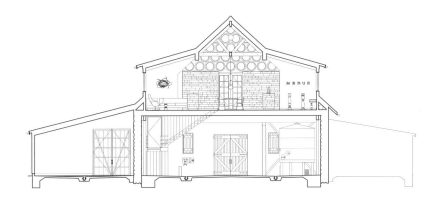

LA CAVE DU VIN 9
Paris, France

Architect | Studio Cyrille Druart
Location | 29, rue du Pont-Neuf, 75001 Paris, France
Year of completion | 2011
Client | private
Type of venue | hospitality
Type of wine | various sorts, selection changes during the year
Number of seating places | 18
Cooling and ventilation techniques | regular air conditioning system
Storage quality | ★ ★ ★ ★ ☆

This design strives to move away from traditional wine bar design and creates a bright, colorful and yet intimate space. Located in the very heart of Paris, La Cave du Vin 9 offers a new type of wine bar – high-end yet within reach. The architects endeavored to break away from conventions, rethinking its space to suit the way people enjoy food and drinks today. Despite being a relative small area, the space is packed with technology. The materials are refined and yet reflect the natural, inherent qualities of the wine itself. One of this project's innovative aspects is that the bar's structure is made of UV-fused glass, raised by a backlit corian top. This element, together with the large abstract mural displaying spilled wine, sends a strong signal that is visible from the street.

La Cave du Vin 9, située au cœur de Paris, renouvelle le concept de bar à vin par sa luminosité, ses riches couleurs et son caractère intime. Les architectes ont cherché à créer un nouveau type de lieu et à structurer l'espace pour qu'il corresponde à la façon dont on aime boire et manger de nos jours. Sur une surface relativement réduite, on trouve ici des équipements high-tech ainsi que des matériaux bruts qui renvoient à la nature raffinée du vin : verre, béton ciré, acier inoxydable et pierre naturelle. Parmi les innovations, citons notamment le bar en verre collé aux ultraviolets et rehaussé d'un plateau en Corian rétro-éclairé. Ce bar constitue un signal fort visible de la rue, au même titre que la grande image murale figurant de manière presque abstraite du vin versé dans un verre.

Der Entwurf distanziert sich von der Gestaltung traditioneller Weinbars und kreiert einen hellen und farbenfrohen, aber auch intimen Raum. Gelegen im Zentrum von Paris, repräsentiert La Cave du Vin 9 einen neuen Typ von Weinbar – hochklassig jedoch nicht abgehoben. Das Bestreben der Architekten war, mit den Konventionen zu brechen, um einen Raum zu schaffen, welcher der heutigen Art des Konsums von Speisen und Getränken gerecht wird. So wurde der relativ kleine Raum mit einer Fülle an Technik ausgestattet. Einer der innovativsten Aspekte ist dabei der aus Quarzglas bestehende Aufbau der Bar mit einem beleuchteten Corian-Aufsatz. Zusammen mit dem übergroßen Foto darüber entsteht so ein starkes visuelles Signal, das sogar von der Straße noch sichtbar ist.

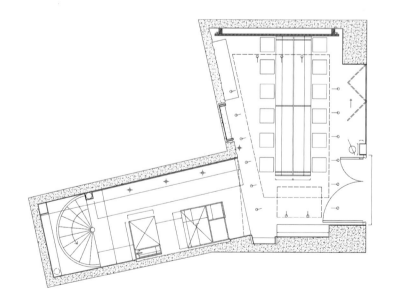

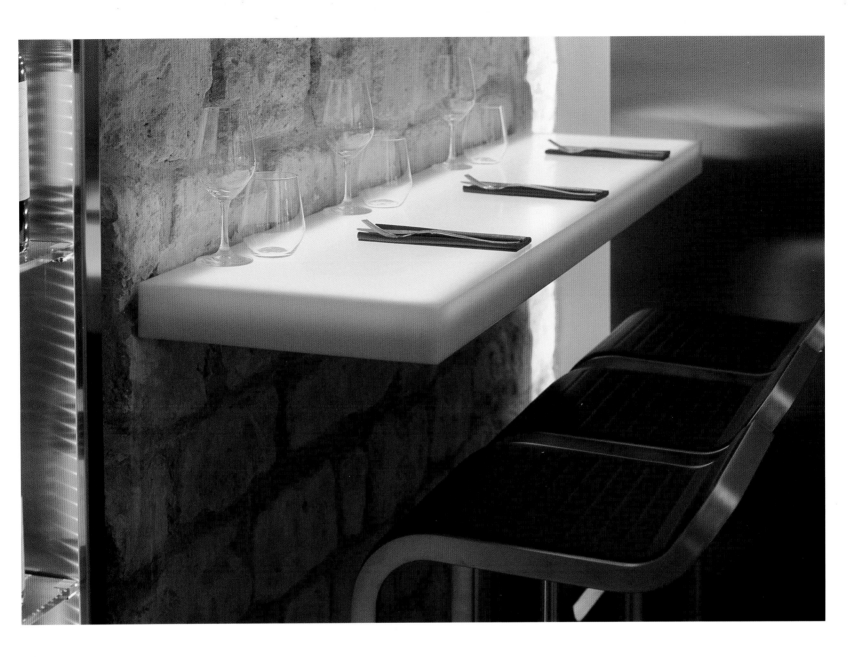

Architect | Ateliers Jean Nouvel
Associated architects | Moon Safari ex-Air Architectes
Landscape architect | OOk Paysagiste
Location | Château La Dominique, 33330 Saint-Émilion, France
Year of completion | 2014
Client | Vignobles Clément Fayat
Type of venue | winery
Type of wine | Merlot, Cabernet Franc, Cabernet Sauvignon
Number of seating places | 100
Cooling and ventilation techniques | cooling system
Trained sommelier | yes
Own vineyard | yes
Storage quality | ★★★★★

CHÂTEAU LA DOMINIQUE
Saint-Émilion, France

Located in the middle of a prestigious vineyard, the Château La Dominique required a design that would bring out and transform this very special landscape. The design concept involved the creation of an object that would rise up out of the existing building and would venture into the vines like a piece of land art. This volume comprises a horizontal plane and four vertical mirror walls. The East and West façades consist of a concrete veil, covered in a set of stainless steel slats that are polished and lacquered a dark red to remind us that, here, it's all about wine. The north façade is transparent, consisting of a large two-way mirror that reflects the vines during the day and then reveals the new fermenting room when night falls.

L'architecte était chargé de construire un nouveau chai à l'architecture audacieuse pour un prestigieux château du Bordelais. Il a donc conçu une extension adossée au bâtiment préexistant, qui domine les vignes à la manière d'une œuvre de « land art ». Les façades est et ouest sont constituées d'un voile en béton recouvert de lames en acier inoxydable peintes en rouge sombre de manière à souligner que tout ici tourne autour du vin. La façade nord se compose quant à elle d'un grand miroir sans tain qui reflète le vignoble durant la journée et laisse entrevoir l'intérieur de la salle de fermentation à la nuit tombée.

Der Entwurf für die Erweiterung des renommierten Weingutes Château La Dominque sollte das inmitten der Reben gelegene Gebäude klar hervorheben. Aus dem existierenden Gebäude wächst ein Objekt hervor, das sich wie ein Land Art-Kunstwerk in die Weinfelder erstreckt. Das Volumen wird durch eine horizontale Ebene und vier verspiegelte Wände begrenzt. Die Betonwände der Ost- und Westfassade sind mit rot lackierten, polierten Edelstahlplatten verkleidet, die auf das Thema Wein verweisen. Die Nordfassade wurde durch zwei große verspiegelte Fenster transparent gestaltet, in denen sich tagsüber die umliegenden Rebstöcke widerspiegeln und die nachts den Blick in den Gärraum ermöglichen.

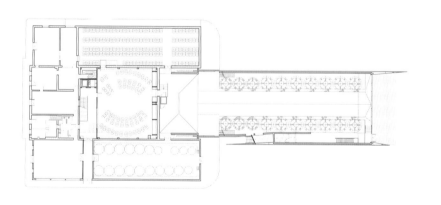

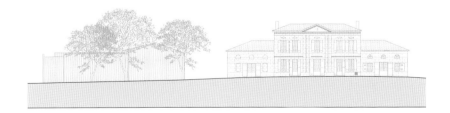

Interior Designer | landau + kindelbacher Architekten Innenarchitekten

Location | Oberlech 50, Lech, Austria

Year of completion | 2012

Client | Signa

Type of venue | hospitality

Type of wine | 1959 Cheval Blanc, 1982 La Tache Grand Cru, 2005 Chateau Palmer, 1989 Chateau Haut Brion, 2005 Chateau Pavi

Number of seating places | 8–10

Trained sommelier | yes

Storage quality | ★★★★☆

CHALET N
Oberlech, Austria

This six-star chalet in glamorous Lech is located in the heart of the Alps and surrounded by a fascinating mountain landscape. The majestic effect of the mountain panorama in the middle of the Arlberg skiing region during the winter, and surrounded by fragrant meadow during the summer, really give this place a sense of magic. The mixture of traditional architecture and high-end interior design both contribute to the exclusive ambience. The use of regional materials combined with modern technology, fixtures and fittings provide guests with a high level of comfort. The large spa area offers the perfect place to escape from everyday life.

Ce chalet six étoiles se trouve à Lech, station alpine de grand luxe implantée dans un site magnifique : les sommets enneigés du massif de l'Arlberg affirment leur majesté en hiver, tandis que les alpages dégagent un parfum envoûtant dès que vient l'été. À ces atouts liés au site s'ajoute le charme d'un intérieur combinant à merveille style traditionnel et design haut de gamme. Le chalet se distingue par l'usage de matériaux d'origine locale associés à des équipements high-tech, ainsi que par un vaste espace bien-être offrant des conditions de relaxation idéales.

Dieses Sechssternechalet liegt im glamourösen Wintersportort Lech, im Herzen der Alpen umgeben von einer faszinierenden Bergwelt. Die majestätische Wirkung des Gipfelpanoramas, inmitten des weitläufigen Skigebiets des Arlbergs im Winter und den duftenden Bergwiesen im Sommer, machen den besonderen Zauber des Ortes aus. Die Mischung aus traditionellem Baustil und hochklassiger Innenarchitektur tut ihr Übriges zum exklusiven Ambiente. Die Verwendung von regionalen Materialien, kombiniert mit modernster Ausstattung und Technik, sorgt für höchsten Komfort, während das großzügige Spa den perfekten Raum bietet, um der Hektik des Alltags zu entfliehen.

126

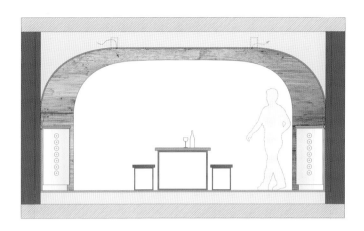

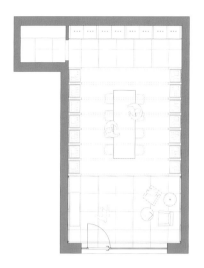

Architect | Fernando Moral Andrés/Moral Arquitectura
Location | Calle Las Bodegas, 34349 Moratinos, Spain
Year of completion | 2012
Client | El Castillo de Moratinos
Type of venue | hospitality
Type of wine | Tierra de León, Bierzo, Ribera del Duero
Number of seating places | 70
Cooling and ventilation techniques | passive cooling techniques
Storage quality | ★★★★☆

CASTLE WINERY
Moratinos, Spain

This new building has been constructed above a wine vault, an old underground gallery housing the restaurant. The new building provides space for the bar, kitchens, and additional secondary spaces. The old vault was carved out of the rock by hand, which gives it a unique rough appearance, while the new building uses natural material such as wood, concrete and bricks, establishing a dialogue with its rural surroundings. The dark vault is illuminated by a series of hanging lights, and subtle niche lighting to create the desired atmosphere.

Un bâtiment moderne abritant un bar, des cuisines et divers espaces fonctionnels a été construit au-dessus de caves voûtées jadis taillées à la main dans la pierre et aujourd'hui aménagées en restaurant. Les caves ont un cachet brut qui forme un contraste saisissant avec l'aspect lisse du bâtiment moderne. Construit en matériaux naturels tels que le bois, la brique et le béton, celui-ci s'intègre parfaitement à son environnement. L'éclairage du niveau inférieur se fait par des lampes nues accrochées au sommet de la voûte et par des dispositifs plus subtils qui mettent en valeur les niches latérales.

Dieser Neubau wurde über einem ehemaligen Weinkeller errichtet, welcher nun ein Restaurant beherbergt. Er bietet Platz für eine Bar, die Küche und weitere Multifunktionsbereiche. Um in einen Dialog mit der Umgebung und dem alten, aus dem massiven Stein von Hand herausgemeißelten Weinkeller zu treten, wurden für den Neubau nur natürliche Materialien wie Holz, Beton und Backstein verwendet. Die einfachen Hängelampen und eine dezente indirekte Beleuchtung in den Nischen unterstreichen die einmalige rustikale Atmosphäre des Weinkellers.

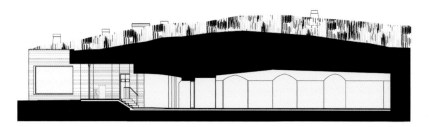

130

131

Architect | Claro + Westendarp Arquitectos
Location | Fundo Quinta de Maipo, Buin, Région Metropolitana, Chile
Year of completion | 2012
Client | Viña Maipo
Type of venue | hospitality
Type of wine | Cabernet Sauvignon, Carmenérè
Number of seating places | 20
Cooling and ventilation techniques | convection, air conditioning
Trained sommelier | yes
Own vineyard | yes
Storage quality | ★★★★☆

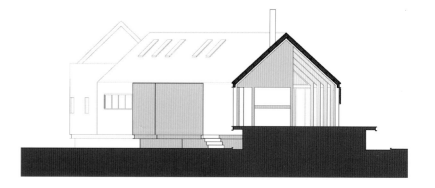

CASA DE HUÉSPEDES – VIÑA MAIPO
Buin, Chile

This project was born out of the desire to create a new building to receive visitors, particularly clients and journalists. The design responds to the rural surroundings, with a saddle roof that reflects the sloping peaks of the nearby mountains and the use of natural materials such as wood. The slight bend in the arrangement of the two separate volumes mimics the line of the hill behind the building. The tasting room, living and dining areas, and terrace are all arranged in sequence along the length of the building.

Les propriétaires du vignoble ont demandé aux architectes de concevoir une structure destinée à accueillir clients et journalistes. Le nouveau bâtiment, qui fait largement usage de matériaux naturels tels que le bois et est couvert par un toit à deux pentes évoquant les collines alentour, se fond harmonieusement dans son environnement rural. Cela d'autant plus que le léger décalage d'alignement des deux volumes correspond au tracé des collines se dressant à l'arrière-plan. Les différents espaces (terrasse, séjour, salle à manger et salle de dégustation) se succèdent les uns derrière les autres dans cet ensemble tout en longueur.

Das Projekt umfasste den Entwurf eines Empfangsgebäudes für Besucher, insbesondere für Journalisten und potentielle Kunden. Um in einen Dialog mit der ländlichen Umgebung zu treten, wurde auf natürliche Materialien wie Holz und ein Satteldach zurückgegriffen, welches Bezug zu den nahe gelegenen Bergen nimmt. Die leichte Krümmung in der Anordnung der beiden Gebäudekörper folgt dem Verlauf der Bergkette dahinter. Durch den lang gestreckten Grundriss wurden der Verkostungsraum, der Wohn- und Essbereich sowie die Terrasse als Sequenz nacheinander angeordnet.

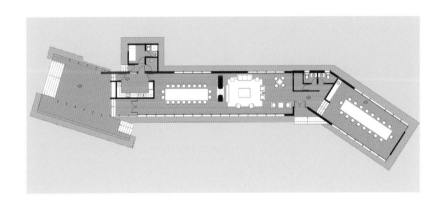

WEINGUT JULIUS
Bobenheim-Roxheim, Germany

This former fire station has been transformed into a winery. A key focus of the design was the creation of a tasting room that expresses the character of the white wine. The use of local stone establishes a playful contrast to the wooden flooring and in-built white units, giving the room a new rectangular character and lightness. The bands of ceiling and wall cladding are characterized by circular openings, which are either artificially illuminated or glazed. Circular showcases for the wine respond to the lighting design. The wine-red fire station entrance permits clear views inside, awakening curiosity and interest from passersby and visitors alike.

Le propriétaire a chargé les architectes de transformer en vinothèque l'ancien poste de pompiers du domaine viticole. L'idée de base était de créer un espace évoquant le caractère particulier du vin blanc. C'est pourquoi on a privilégié la pierre calcaire locale et les murs blancs, qui confèrent à l'espace légèreté et linéarité. Des découpes circulaires plus ou moins grandes pratiquées au plafond et dans les murs assurent l'éclairage naturel et artificiel de l'intérieur, tout en établissant un lien entre tradition et modernité. D'autres découpes sont utilisées pour mettre des bouteilles en valeur. Les architectes ont conservé la porte rouge du poste de pompiers pour sa capacité à susciter la curiosité des visiteurs.

Auf Wunsch der Bauherren wurde das ehemalige Feuerwehrgerätehaus in eine Vinothek umgenutzt. Grundgedanke war, einen Verkostungsraum zu schaffen, der den Charakter der Weißweine auch räumlich zum Ausdruck bringt. Die Wand aus lokalem Bruchstein verleiht dem Raum im Zusammenspiel mit Massivholzboden und Einbauten in kühlem Weiß eine neue Leichtigkeit und Geradlinigkeit. Maßgeblich ist eine bandförmige Decken- und Wandverkleidung, deren kreisförmige Ausschnitte für Kunst- und Tageslichtbeleuchtung sorgen. Sie symbolisiert eine Verbindung aus Tradition und Moderne. Ebenfalls kreisförmig ausgeschnittene Präsentationsflächen für die Weine bilden das Pendant zur Beleuchtung. Das Weinrot des Feuerwehrtores gewährt Passanten und Besuchern gleichermaßen einen Einblick und weckt Neugierde auf das Raumgefühl im Innern.

Architect | Raum & Architektur / Christiane Jeromin
Location | Gerhart-Hauptmann-Straße 37,
67240 Bobenheim-Roxheim, Germany
Year of completion | 2008
Client | Georg Julius
Type of venue | winery
Type of wine | Sauvignon blanc, Riesling,
Pinot gris, Pinot Blanc, Pinot Noir, Dornfelder, Merlot
Number of seating places | 12
Own vineyard | yes
Storage quality | ★★★★☆

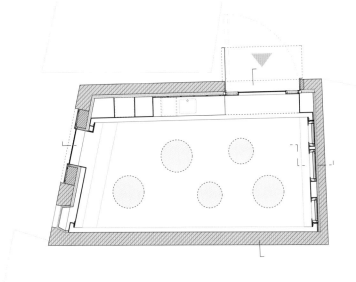

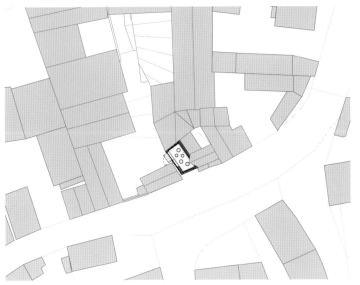

Architect | mode:lina architekci
Location | Czechosłowacka 106, 61476 Poznan, Poland
Year of completion | 2014
Client | Fiesta del Vino
Type of venue | hospitality
Number of seating places | 20
Trained sommelier | yes
Storage quality | ★★★☆☆

FIESTA DEL VINO WINE BAR
Poznan, Poland

This project involved designing a wine shop with a tapas bar and tasting area. The entire space is clearly divided into various areas that nevertheless come together to form a coherent whole. The exterior is fitted with a white wooden lattice that is reminiscent of wine crates, signifying the function of the store. A range of warm colors characterizes the interior design; a warm and welcoming brown, complemented by red, blue and white. The design is functional yet striking, signifying its exclusivity and creating a high-quality space for the products within.

Le projet portait ici sur la réalisation d'une vinothèque avec salle de dégustation et bar à tapas. Les architectes ont structuré l'espace en délimitant plusieurs secteurs conçus pour former un tout. Le parement de façade utilisant des planches peintes en blanc rappelle les caisses de vin traditionnelles et indique ainsi d'emblée la fonction du bâtiment. L'intérieur est plus riche en couleurs puisqu'on y trouve des teintes chaudes telles que le brun et le rouge, auxquelles s'ajoutent des teintes froides telles que le bleu et le blanc. Bien que fonctionnelle, la décoration intérieure est remarquable en ce qu'elle excelle à mettre en valeur les vins proposés à la vente.

Die Gestaltung dieses Weingeschäfts sollte gleichzeitig eine Tapasbar und einen Bereich für Weinproben umfassen. Der gesamte Raum wurde dazu in einzelne Sektionen gegliedert, die zusammengenommen ein geschlossenes Ganzes bilden. Die Verkleidung der Fassade aus weißen Holzlatten spielt auf traditionelle Weinkisten an und verweist somit auf die Funktion des Geschäfts. Die Farbpalette des Innenraums zeichnet sich durch warme Töne aus: von einem warmen, einladenden Braun, über Rot und Blau bis hin zu Weiß. Die Inneneinrichtung ist funktional gehalten, besticht jedoch durch ihr Design, welches durch seine Exklusivität eine angemessene Umgebung zur Präsentation der Produkte schafft.

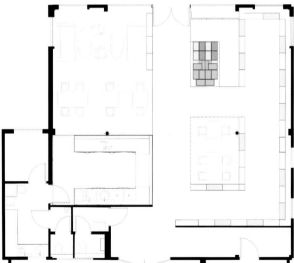

144

Architect | Spitzbart + partners
Artists | Markus Spitzbart, Rüdiger Fritz, Jörg Hoffmann, Alexander Schleissing
Location | Steinbichlstraße 3, 4812 Pinsdorf, Austria
Year of completion | 2014
Client | Gabriele, Wolfgang and Patrick Steiner
Type of venue | hospitality
Number of seating places | 103
Storage quality | ★★★☆☆

146

STEINER'S
Pinsdorf, Austria

Well-executed architecture can function like an advertisement for an entire region. This restaurant and wine bar has undergone a complete transformation, creating a location that is large, modern and yet comfortable. The interior design combines niches, large tables and seating along the bar. Unusual details, such as a baldachin in the café, and the red flooring in the wine bar come together to create a unique space longing to be experienced with all the senses. The varied culinary service includes everything from breakfast, to light lunch, Mediterranean meals, regional specialties and even cake and ice cream from Steiner's own confectionary.

Une architecture de qualité peut contribuer à l'image de marque de toute une région. Tel est le cas de ce restaurant/bar à vin récemment modernisé qui brille désormais par son caractère vaste et confortable. Les clients peuvent au choix s'asseoir au bar ou s'attabler au restaurant, ces différents espaces se caractérisant par des détails tels que des baldaquins ou du parquet rouge qui contribuent à l'atmosphère particulière du lieu. Le restaurant, ouvert toute la journée, sert des spécialités méditerranéennes et régionales ainsi que des gâteaux et des glaces de fabrication maison.

Gute Architektur kann als Aushängeschild einer ganzen Region dienen. Dieses Restaurant mit angeschlossener Weinbar wurde einem kompletten Umbau unterzogen, um eine moderne Atmosphäre zu schaffen, die durch Großzügigkeit und Komfort besticht. Die Innenarchitektur verbindet private Nischen mit großen Tischen und Sitzgelegenheiten an der Bar. Zugleich wurde mit speziellen Details wie einem Baldachin im Cafébereich und dem roten Fußboden in der Weinbar Orte des Erlebens und der Inszenierung geschaffen. Die kulinarische Vielfalt erstreckt sich über das gesamte Tagesangebot und umfasst neben mediterranen Speisen auch regionale Spezialitäten sowie Eis und Kuchen aus der hauseigenen Produktion.

Architect | Kokaistudios
Location | Leighton Road, Tongluowan, Hong Kong, China
Year of completion | 2012
Client | Altaya etc wine shops
Type of venue | retail
Number of seating places | 10
Type of wine | Bordeaux
Trained sommelier | yes
Storage quality | ★★★★☆

ALTAYA ETC WINE SHOPS
– BORDEAUX ETC
Hong Kong, China

Kokaistudios have designed two thematic etc wine shops, a new brand created by high-end wine distributor Altaya in Hong Kong. Altaya etc wine shops – Bordeaux etc is characterized by the striking contrast between the sharp white walls and black shelving and fittings. The entire space is illuminated by bright white lighting strips integrated into the ceiling and walls. A decorative fire at the center of the store adds a welcoming and comfortable touch to the modern design. The space also offers a number of seating options, where visitors can sit and enjoy a wine tasting session. The entire design is simple and elegant, allowing the products to take center stage.

Le bureau d'architectes Kokaistudios a conçu deux magasins pour le marchand de vin haut de gamme Altaya implanté à Hong Kong. Celui présenté ici se caractérise par un contraste entre les murs blancs et le mobilier noir, le tout étant fortement éclairé par des bandes lumineuses blanches intégrées aux murs et au plafond. Un feu de cheminée virtuel « brûlant » au centre de l'espace ajoute une touche traditionnelle à la décoration moderniste. On trouve également à l'intérieur de nombreux sièges qui invitent les clients à déguster le vin en toute sérénité. Ce design tout en retenue et d'une élégante simplicité accorde une place de choix aux vins proposés à la vente.

Kokaistudios entwarfen zwei Themengeschäfte für die neue etc Weinladenkette des auf hochwertige Weine spezialisierten Händlers Altaya in Hong Kong. Bordeaux etc wird durch den wirkungsvollen Kontrast zwischen weißen Wänden und den schwarzen Regalen und Einbauten charakterisiert. Der gesamte Raum wird durch helle Lichtbänder beleuchtet, die in der Decke und in den Wänden eingelassen wurden. Ein dekorativer Kamin in der Mitte des Geschäfts bildet ein wohnliches Gegengewicht zu dem modernen Design. Die Räumlichkeiten beherbergen zudem mehrere Sitzgelegenheiten für Weinproben. Der Gesamtcharakter der Weinhandlung ist einfach und elegant; die Weine stehen im Mittelpunkt.

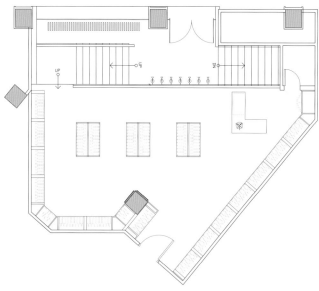

THE TASTINGS ROOM
Singapore, Singapore

Architect | Studio SKLIM
Location | 01-08 Marina Square, 039594 Singapore, Singapore
Year of completion | 2011
Client | Envis Group
Type of venue | hospitality
Type of wine | new and old world wines
Number of seating places | 68
Cooling and ventilation techniques | Eurocave Air-Con system in cellar
Trained sommelier | yes
Storage quality | ★★★★☆

The Tastings Room is a new addition to the heart of Singapore's Central Business District. The restaurant's vision was to refresh the perception of wine and food culture in Singapore by providing them at affordable prices. The overall spatial experience sandwiches the crafted black volumes between the exposed ceiling and concrete screed floor. The programmatic composition was divided into three main areas; wine, bistro and shared wine and bistro spaces. The central bar sits firmly in the middle and negotiates the needs of both the wine area and bistro, as well as providing the point of sale for this establishment.

Ce nouveau restaurant vient d'être construit au cœur du quartier des affaires de Singapour, avec pour objectif de renouveler l'image du vin et de la bonne cuisine en les mettant à portée d'un plus large public. La décoration se caractérise par des murs noirs, un sol en béton brut de coffrage et un plafond laissant voir les équipements techniques. L'intérieur est structuré en trois espaces différents (bistro, magasin de vins et espace mixte), avec au centre un comptoir regroupant toutes les opérations de vente.

Das Restaurant The Tastings Room eröffnete im Herzen von Singapurs Central Business District mit dem Konzept, die Wein- und Esskultur in Singapur durch erschwingliche Preise zu fördern. Der Raum wird durch die schwarzen Volumina dominiert, welche mit der freigelegten Decke und dem Betonboden kontrastieren und nachträglich eingebaut wurden. Die Aufteilung erfolgte in drei Hauptbereiche nach Nutzung: Bistro, Wein- und gemischter Bereich. Um zwischen dem Bistro und dem Weinbereich zu vermitteln und die Anforderungen beider Bereiche abzudecken, wurde eine Bar in der Mitte des Raumes installiert, wo sie gut sichtbar als Hauptverkaufsstelle dient.

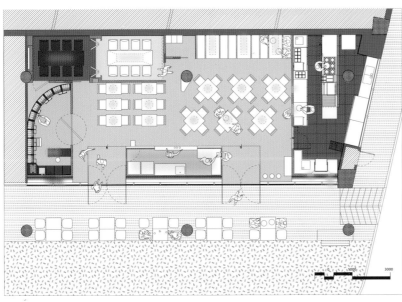

DIVINO NORDHEIM
Nordheim, Germany

Divino vinothek belongs to a winegrowers' cooperative in Nordheim, Germany and has been conceived as an extension of the existing premises. Wine produced on-site and a range of other products from the region, are displayed in the light-flooded building. Natural materials such as wood from fruit trees and local natural stone characterize the entire interior design and help to create the pleasing atmosphere. In addition to the large tasting counter, visitors can also make use of the relaxing wine lounge, seminar space and event area. A café bistro with terrace is located in the tranquil courtyard and offers light meals and alternative drinks. An exhibition area located on the gallery accommodates art exhibitions and also offers visitors the chance to make use of the library and internet portals.

La vinothèque Divino est venue récemment compléter la coopérative viticole de Nordheim. Il s'agit d'un bâtiment très lumineux affecté à la vente de vins et autres produits du terroir. Des matériaux naturels tels que la pierre d'origine locale et du bois d'arbres fruitiers y génèrent une atmosphère accueillante. L'espace disponible est occupé par un salon, plusieurs salles de conférences et une salle de dégustation équipée d'un grand comptoir. On y trouve également un bistro avec terrasse servant des repas légers et des boissons « alternatives », ainsi qu'une salle accueillant des expositions temporaires et une médiathèque spécialisée sur le thème du vin et de la vigne.

Die Vinothek Divino der Winzergenossenschaft Nordheim wurde als Anbau an den bestehenden Genossenschaftsbetrieb konzipiert. In dem lichtdurchfluteten Gebäude werden der hauseigene Wein sowie ländliche Produkte aus der Region präsentiert. Natürliche Materialien wie edle Obstbaum-Hölzer und lokaler Naturstein prägen die im ganzen Gebäude vorherrschende, ansprechende Atmosphäre. Neben der großzügigen Probiertheke erwarten den Besucher eine Wein-Lounge sowie Seminar- und Veranstaltungsräume. Ein Café-Bistro mit Terrasse im ruhigen Winzerhof bietet kleine Speisen und alternative Getränke an. Im Ausstellungsbereich auf der Galerie finden wechselnde Kunstausstellungen statt. Hier kann sich der Besucher in der Bibliothek und an Internet-Plätzen über das Thema Wein informieren.

Architect | Frank + Stirnweiss Architekten
Interior architect | Andreas Weber Architektur +
Design, Barbara Adelmann-Weber
Location | Langgasse 33, 97334 Nordheim, Germany
Year of completion | 2004
Client | Winzergenossenschaft Nordheim
Type of venue | retail
Type of wine | Pinot Noir, Pinot Blanc, Bacchus,
Silvaner, Müller-Thurgau, Chardonnay, Riesling
Number of seating places | 120
Trained sommelier | yes
Own vineyard | yes
Storage quality | ★★★☆☆

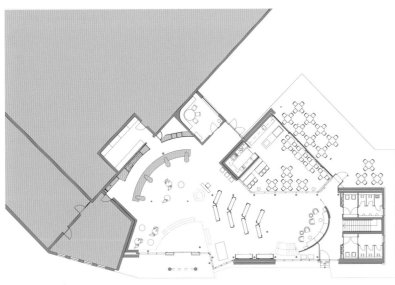

Architect | Ekler Architect
Location | 8481 Somlóvásárhely, Hungary
Year of completion | 2012
Client | Kreinbacher Champagne Winery Ltd., Szent Ilona Winery Ltd.
Type of venue | winery
Type of wine | Juhfark, Syrah, Nagy-Somlói, Furmint, Hárslevelű, Öreg Tőkék Bora wine blends, sparkling wines
Number of seating places | 70
Cooling and ventilation techniques | fan-coil, humidifier
Trained sommelier | yes
Own vineyard | yes
Storage quality | ★★★★☆

164

SOMLÓ WINERY COMPLEX
Somlóvásárhely, Hungary

Budapest-based practice Ekler Architect constructed the first phase of this winery complex in the Hungarian wine region Somló. The two volumes containing the traditional winery and a winery for the production of sparkling wine are part of a larger development. From the approach they are concealed by an artificial hill that blends in with the topography of Somló Mountain. The monolithic concrete masses evoke forms of geological forces with layouts reminiscent of the shape of lava flows. The cantilevered structure protruding from the hill-form of the winery houses the tasting room for visitors and offers panoramic views over the countryside.

Le bureau d'architectes Ekler, implanté à Budapest, a réalisé la première phase de travaux de ce complexe viticole de la région de Somló. Elle portait sur la construction de deux bâtiments de production, l'un pour le vin, l'autre pour le mousseux. On ne les distingue pas de loin car ils sont masqués derrière un monticule artificiel qui se confond avec les collines environnantes. De plus près, on remarque des monolithes de béton qui ne sont pas sans évoquer des coulées de lave solidifiées, ainsi qu'une structure en porte-à-faux qui abrite une salle de dégustation offrant une vue panoramique sur les alentours.

Das Budapester Architekturbüro Ekler war für den Entwurf der ersten Bauphase dieses Weinguts im ungarischen Weinbaugebiet Somló verantwortlich. Die zwei Gebäudekörper beherbergen einen traditionellen Weinkeller und einen zur Herstellung nach Champagnermethode und sind Teil eines größeren Komplexes. Von Weitem erscheinen sie durch einen künstlichen Hügel verdeckt, der sich perfekt in die Landschaft des Berges Somló einfügt, während die monolithischen Betonkörper bei näherer Betrachtung Assoziationen an erkaltete Lavaströme hervorrufen. Das aus dem Hang des Hügels auskragende Gebäudevolumen beherbergt den Verkostungsraum und bietet einen Panoramablick über die umliegende Landschaft.

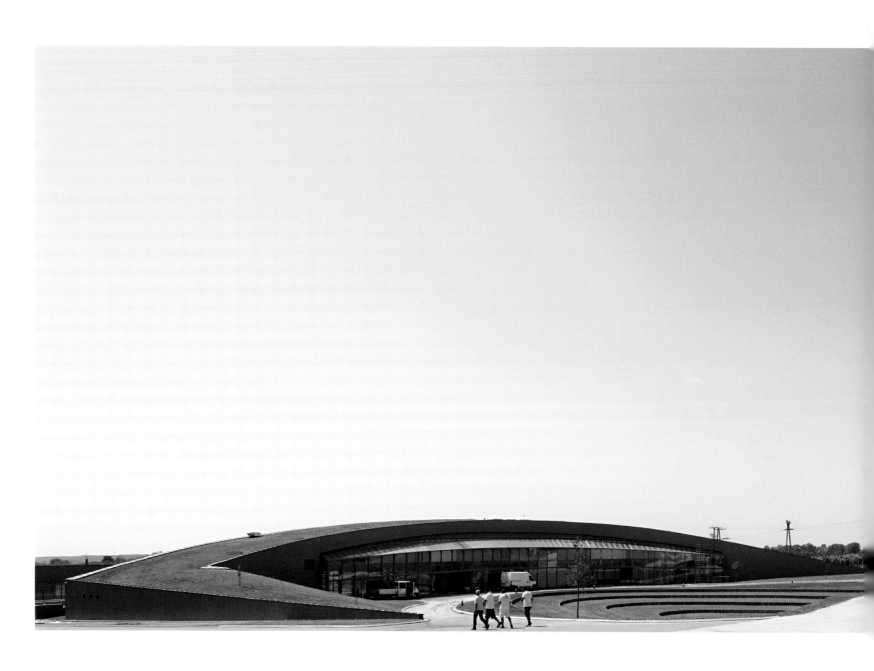

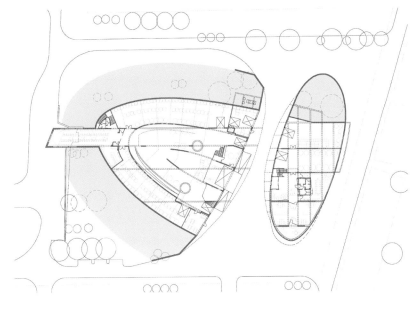

Architect | Freie Architekten Frieß + Moster
Interior architect | Planungsbüro Münzing
Location | Domäne Steinberg, 65346 Eltville, Germany
Year of completion | 2008
Client | Hessische Staatsweingüter GmbH
Type of venue | retail
Type of wine | Riesling, Pinot Noir, Pinot Blanc, Pinot Gris
Number of seating places | 107
Own vineyard | yes
Storage quality | ★★★★☆

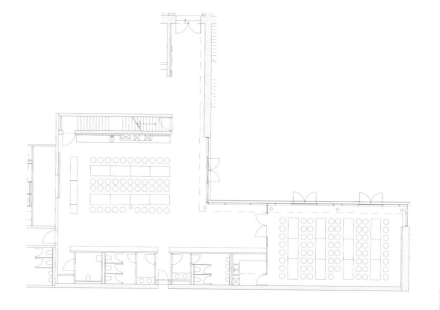

HESSISCHE STAATSWEINGÜTER KLOSTER EBERBACH
Eltville, Germany

The Steinbergkeller, belonging to the Hessische Staatsweingüter (Hessian State Wine Domain) and located in close proximity to the famous Kloster Eberbach, has been built almost completely underground. The architecture seeks to combine design requirements with the desired esthetics, establishing a dialogue with the surrounding landscape. It also responds to the nearby Steinberg Wall and the listed timber frame buildings located on the site. Just a few carefully selected and high-quality materials have been chosen for the interior design. European oak establishes a connection to the wooden vats in the cellar and the process of traditional winemaking.

Le chai du vignoble national de la Hesse, situé à proximité de l'abbaye d'Eberbach produisant un excellent cru, est presque entièrement souterrain. Le style retenu affirme son ambition en matière d'architecture tout en respectant la tradition du vignoble, puisqu'il évoque à la fois la pierre du célèbre mur de Steinberg et les maisons à colombages classées présentes sur le site. La décoration intérieure n'utilise que du béton brut de coffrage et quelques matériaux soigneusement sélectionnés, notamment du chêne établissant un lien direct avec les barriques traditionnelles entreposées dans la cave.

Der Steinbergkeller der Hessischen Staatsweingüter, in unmittelbarer Nähe zu dem in Weinkennerkreisen bekannten Kloster Eberbach gelegen, wurde fast vollständig unterirdisch angelegt. Die Architektur stellt einen Dialog zwischen den gestalterischen Ansprüchen und der vom Weinbau geprägten Kulturlandschaft her und bezieht sich auch auf die nahegelegene Steinbergmauer und die denkmalgeschützten Fachwerkhäuser auf dem Areal. Nur wenige, ausgesuchte hochwertige Materialien wurden zu dem in Sichtbeton erstellten Gebäude kombiniert. Europäische Eiche schafft einen Bezug zu den im Keller lagernden Holzfässern und der Tradition der Weinherstellung.

Architect | March Gut industrial design
Location | Kellergasse, 3408 Feuersbrunn, Austria
Year of completion | 2013
Client | Clemens Strobl
Type of venue | winery
Type of wine | Green Veltliner, Riesling
Number of seating places | approx. 25
Cooling and ventilation techniques | vaulted cellar, air circulation
Trained sommelier | yes
Own vineyard | yes
Storage quality | ★★★★☆

172

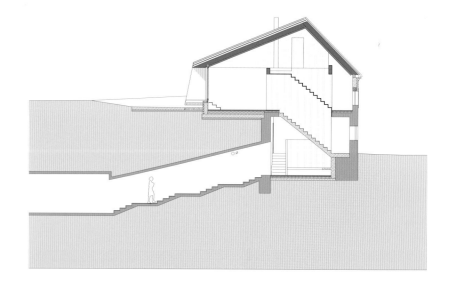

STROBL KELLER
Feuersbrunn, Austria

This former winery belonging to Clemens Strobl in Lower Austria has been transformed into a representative company location and now stretches over four levels. The existing buildings have been maintained but complemented by additional new spaces, creating a striking and welcoming building ensemble. The cellar is comfortable, dimly lit and sound proofed and is characterized by its cozy atmosphere. The first floor is open and light, offering direct views over the vineyard. Despite the limited space available, the rooms appear larger than they are, offering visitors space to relax and taste the wide range of wines on offer.

Au terme de sa rénovation, le chai Clemens Strobl du vignoble de Feuersbrunn, en Basse-Autriche, est désormais un espace commercial de prestige sur quatre niveaux. Le bâti ancien a conservé son aspect authentique et a été complété par des locaux à la décoration soignée. Tous les bâtiments sont insonorisés et rayonnent d'une atmosphère chaleureuse. Le niveau supérieur, particulièrement lumineux, s'ouvre largement sur le vignoble environnant. En dépit d'une surface au sol relativement réduite, les architectes ont su créer ici un ensemble accueillant où il fait bon déguster le cru local.

Der ehemalige Weinkeller der Weinmanufaktur Clemens Strobl im niederösterreichischen Feuersbrunn wurde zum Repräsentationsort des Betriebes umgestaltet und erstreckt sich heute über vier Ebenen. Dabei wurden die alten Gebäudeteile in ihrer Ursprünglichkeit erhalten und um neue Räumlichkeiten ergänzt: Die Weinmanufaktur ist repräsentativ und ansprechend. Der Keller ist behaglich, licht- und schallgedämpft und vermittelt eine gemütliche Atmosphäre. Der erste Stock präsentiert sich offen und hell und ermöglicht einen direkten Blick in die Weinberge. So entstand trotz geringer Quadratmeterzahl ein großzügiges Erscheinungsbild, das den Besucher zum Verweilen und zur Degustation der produzierten Weine einlädt.

ALTAYA ETC WINE SHOPS
– CHAMPAGNE ETC
Hong Kong, China

Architect | Kokaistudios
Location | 19 underground Lyndhurst Central, Hong Kong, China
Year of completion | 2012
Client | Altaya etc wine shops
Type of venue | wine shop
Type of wine | Champagne, sparkling wine
Trained sommelier | yes
Storage quality | ★★★★☆

Champagne etc is part of Altaya etc wine shops, a new high-end wine distributor in Hong Kong. This store is characterized by black shelving and fittings, complemented by white walls and glass elements. The large glass windows act as display cases, drawing curious gazes from passersby and tempting visitors to step inside. The innovative use of empty bottles as decoration helps to relax the seriousness of the design, introducing a quirky element. The simplicity of the design lends the space an almost showroom-like quality, emphasizing the products and avoiding gimmicks.

Altaya est un marchand de vin haut de gamme implanté à Hong Kong. Pour ce second magasin, réservé au champagne, les architectes ont privilégié un mobilier noir, des murs blancs et une façade entièrement en verre qui invite les passants à venir découvrir la gamme des vins proposés. Des bouteilles vides, disposées le goulot en bas comme dans les caves de Champagne, ajoutent une note désinvolte à la décoration somme toute assez austère. Cette simplicité délibérée qui fait fi de tout gadget vise à focaliser l'attention des clients sur les bouteilles.

Champagne etc ist eine Filiale der etc Weinläden von Altaya, einem Weinhändler in Hongkong, der sich auf hochwertige Weine spezialisiert hat. Das Geschäft wird durch schwarze Regale und Einbauten bestimmt, die sich kontrastreich von den weißen Wänden und Glaselementen abheben. Die große Fenster dienen als Präsentationsregale, wodurch die Aufmerksamkeit der Passanten gesteigert und der Anteil der Laufkundschaft erhöht wird. Der innovative Einsatz von leeren Flaschen als herausstechendes Gestaltungselement hilft dabei, die Strenge des Designs aufzubrechen. Die Schlichtheit der Gestaltung verleiht dem Raum eine Showroom ähnliche Atmosphäre, welche das Produkt hervorhebt und unnötige Spielereien vermeidet.

Architect | Scheel|Inselsbacher Architekten + Ingenieure
Location | Wilhelm-Maybach-Straße 25, 71394 Kernen im Remstal, Germany
Year of completion | 2013
Client | Ulrich and Friedrich Kern
Type of venue | winery
Type of wine | mainly regional types of wine
Number of seating places | 100
Own vineyard | yes
Storage quality | ★★★★☆

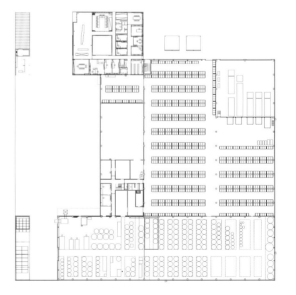

WEINKELLER WILHELM KERN
Kernen im Remstal, Germany

The Wilhelm Kern wine cellar is a new construction located on the edge of the Kernen im Remstal winegrowing region and draws all the operational facilities together in one place. In addition to the cellar and logistics, the presentation and sales area also play a key role in the design. In the direction of the Remstal vineyards to the south and west the site borders on agricultural land. The sales area also features an outdoor area for tasting and events, and from here one can see the operational areas where the wine is produced. The administration areas and sales building, bottling area and cellar offices are all clad with wood. The arrangement of the wooden façade cladding is reminiscent of the silhouette of the surrounding vineyards.

La société viticole Wilhelm Kern a fait construire ce bâtiment à la périphérie du village de Kernen im Remstal afin d'y regrouper toutes les opérations de vinification et de commercialisation. La logistique, la présentation et la vente du vin y occupent une place de premier plan. Le bâtiment est directement bordé par le vignoble à l'ouest et au sud, de sorte que les visiteurs se sentent en contact direct avec la magie du vin lorsqu'ils sont dans l'espace de vente ou participent aux séances de dégustation organisées sur l'esplanade. Les bureaux et la salle de mise en bouteilles se trouvent derrière l'enveloppe en bois dont les ajours évoquent la silhouette des coteaux environnants.

Um alle Betriebsteile an einem Ort zusammenzuführen, wurde der Neubau des Weinkellers Wilhelm Kern am Ortsrand der Weinbaugemeinde Kernen im Remstal errichtet. Neben Keller und Logistik kommt dem Präsentations- und Verkaufsbereich eine zentrale Bedeutung zu. Südlich und westlich des Richtung der Remstaler Weinberge ausgerichteten Geländes befinden sich landwirtschaftlich genutzte Flächen. Von den Verkaufsräumen mit Außenbereichen zur Verkostung und für Veranstaltungen hat man dezenten Einblick in die Bereiche der Weinproduktion. Das Verwaltungs- und Verkaufsgebäude sowie die Abfüllung mit Kellerbüros sind mit einer Holzverschalung verkleidet, die an die Silhouette der umliegenden Weinberge erinnert.

Architect | Spitzbart + partners
Artists | Markus Spitzbart, Michael Maier, Jörg Hoffmann, Alexander Schleissing
Location | Am Cobenzl 96, 1190 Vienna, Austria
Year of completion | 2010
Client | City Administration of Vienna
Type of venue | winery
Type of wine | Vienna field blend, Green Veltiner, Riesling, Muscat Blanc à Petits Grains, Pinot
Blanc, Cabernet Sauvignon, Merlot, Pinot Noir, Blauer Zweigelt, sparkling wine
Number of seating places | approx. 15
Own vineyard | yes
Storage quality | ★★★★☆

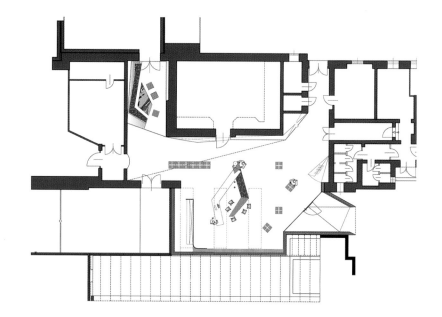

WEINGUT DER STADT WIEN COBENZL
Vienna, Austria

Approximately 230 winegrowers cultivate high-quality wine on this 700-hectar site on the outskirts of the city, funded by the city of Vienna. The Cobenzl winery itself is operated by the city. The new design of the tasting area has created a modern, charismatic and multifunctional space in the midst of traditional architecture: The space is also suitable for events such as weddings. High-quality materials such as corian, acacia and large impressive pictures characterize the ambience of the large room.

Parmi les 230 vignerons qui cultivent les sept cents hectares de vignes répartis autour de Vienne, certains travaillent pour le domaine de Cobenzl, réputé pour son cru et directement géré par la municipalité de la capitale autrichienne. La rénovation de la salle de dégustation du domaine a permis de réaliser, dans un bâtiment traditionnel, un espace moderne et multifonctionnel qui peut accueillir un grand nombre d'invités, par exemple à l'occasion d'un mariage. Cette grande salle doit son atmosphère particulière à des matériaux nobles (notamment le Corian), ainsi qu'à des agrandissements photographiques assez impressionnants.

Auf den Rebflächen am Stadtrand bauen rund 230 Winzer auf 700 Hektar ihren Qualitätswein an. Gefördert werden sie von der Stadt Wien, die mit dem Weingut Cobenzl selbst eines der führenden Weingüter bewirtschaftet. Durch die Neugestaltung des Degustationsraumes entstand inmitten traditioneller Architektur ein moderner, charismatischer und multifunktioneller Ort, der auch Veranstaltungen, beispielsweise Hochzeiten, den passenden Rahmen bietet. Edlen Materialen wie Corian, gedämpfte Akazie und große stimmungsvolle Bilder prägen das Ambiente des großzügigen Raums.

WINZER KREMS
Krems, Austria

Architects | architektur krammer
Location | Sandgrube 13, 3500 Krems, Austria
Year of completion | 2005
Client | Winzer Krems
Type of venue | winery
Own vineyard | yes
Storage quality | ★★★☆☆

The new press building forms the most striking part of this newly designed complex, with a curving roof that makes it recognizable from afar. Key focuses of the design included the provision of plenty of daylight inside the building and simplified operation processes for delivery and handling goods. The glass façade allows visitors a glimpse of modern wine production. The new winery complex is adopted from the original buildings. The architects were faced with the challenge of combining the relatively conservative existing buildings with new modern elements. This project makes the connections between wine, art and architecture tangible. Artworks from Georgia Creimer and Karl Korab complete the design.

Les bâtiments anciens de ce complexe viticole ont été récemment rénovés et complétés par un pressoir au toit légèrement incurvé visible de loin. L'architecte s'est efforcé d'optimiser l'éclairage naturel et de simplifier le passage entre les différentes étapes de production, tout en reliant le nouvel édifice au bâti ancien. Au terme des travaux de modernisation, ce chai et son pressoir aux façades en verre offrent une approche radicalement nouvelle du monde du vin et permettent au public d'apprécier directement les différents procédés de production mis en œuvre. Deux artistes, Georgia Creimer et Karl Korab, ont par ailleurs contribué, grâce à leur talent, à la richesse artistique de cet ensemble qui établit un lien entre vin et architecture.

Auffälligstes Gebäude dieses umgestalteten Komplexes ist das neue Presshaus, welches durch sein geschwungenes Dach als Zeichen weithin in der Landschaft sichtbar ist. Die Zufuhr von Tageslicht sowie die Vereinfachung der Anlieferung und der Produktionsabläufe waren die grundlegenden Prinzipien bei der Neugestaltung des Ensembles. Dabei musste eine Brücke zwischen dem eher biederen Bestand und den Erfordernissen eines modernen Weingutes geschlagen werden. Dies wurde unter anderem durch die Schaffung der neuen Weinerlebniswelt erreicht und durch die Glasfassaden, die einen direkten Einblick in die Weinproduktion ermöglichen. Die Verbindung zwischen Wein, Kunst und Architektur wurde bei diesem Projekt auf besondere Weise erreicht und gelebt. Georgia Creimer und Karl Korab bereichern und ergänzen mit ihren Kunstwerken die Gestaltung.

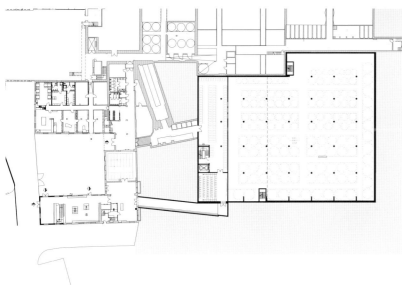

Architect | Baurconsult Architekten Ingenieure
Location | Marktplatz 1, 97475 Zeil am Main, Germany
Year of completion | 2010
Client | Roger Nüßlein
Type of venue | retail
Type of wine | Müller-Thurgau, Silvaner, Riesling, Pinot Blanc, Scheurebe, Bacchus, Domina,
Pinot Noir, Dornfelder
Number of seating places | 60–70
Trained sommelier | yes
Own vineyard | yes
Storage quality | ★★★★★

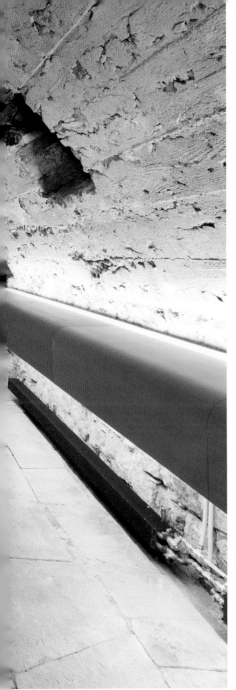

WEINHAUS NÜSSLEIN
Zeil am Main, Germany

Motivated by a generation change, this traditional family business expressed the wish to devise new marketing ideas that would attract additional target groups. Typical elements of the winemaking process flow into the design: the walls are decorated with wine bottles displayed on backlit wooden panels, complemented by the presentation of selected grape varieties. The existing floors, walls and ceilings in the oldest part of the building have been restored and combined with new custom-made furnishings. Highlight is the barrel-vaulted cellar, where a long ash counter is used for wine tasting sessions. The entire design is dominated by reduced, subtle forms and natural materials.

À l'occasion d'un renouvellement de génération, le nouveau propriétaire du domaine viticole Nüsslein souhaitait apporter des modifications aux bâtiments afin d'élargir sa clientèle. Les architectes ont intégré à leur concept des éléments typiques de la viticulture, notamment des bouteilles rétroéclairées sur panneaux de bois qui servent soit de décoration, soit de présentoirs pour les différents crus. Dans la partie la plus ancienne du bâtiment, le sol, les murs et le plafond ont retrouvé leur aspect d'origine et sont en parfaite harmonie avec le mobilier moderne spécialement conçu. La grande cave voûtée, pourvue d'une longue table en frêne servant à la dégustation, est particulièrement impressionnante. Comme toutes les autres pièces, elle se distingue par sa sobriété et la priorité qu'elle accorde aux matériaux naturels.

Angeregt durch einen Generationenwechsel möchte das traditionsreiche Familienunternehmen Weinhaus Nüßlein mit neuen Vermarktungsideen zusätzliche Zielgruppen erschließen. Typische Elemente des Weinbaus flossen in den Entwurf ein: Die Wände sind mit Weinflaschen auf hinterleuchteten Paneelen dekoriert, zudem werden in besonderen Bereichen ausgewählte Rebsorten präsentiert. Im ältesten Gebäudeteil wurden die bestehenden Boden-, Wand- und Deckenbeläge restauriert und mit eigens entworfenem Mobiliar kombiniert. Der Gewölbekeller bildet den Höhepunkt: An einer langen Eschentafel können Weine verkostet werden. In allen Räumen dominieren reduzierte Formen und natürliche Materialien.

197

WEINGUT KOPPIISCH
Neusiedl am See, Austria

This project involved transforming the existing tasting area and additional extensions into a modern and unified building ensemble. Although the restructuring is visible, the old down-to-earth character of the existing buildings is still clearly discernible. In order to optimize operational processes, the entire cellar has been dug 50 centimeters deeper. The tasting area is characterized by the use of white oiled wood; the wide wooden panels and the corner bench lend the space an air of comfort and security. Industrial lamps and modular tables give the space the desired flexibility. In order to give the design a unified appearance, a large section of the façade has been clad with spruce boards.

Les architectes étaient chargés de moderniser un bâtiment de production et de dégustation en veillant à ce que le nouveau n'entre pas en conflit avec l'ancien. Afin de simplifier les processus de production, la profondeur de la cave a été augmentée de cinquante centimètres. La salle de dégustation se caractérise par ses boiseries recouvertes de lasure blanche, son parquet à larges lames également peint en blanc, et une banquette qui court le long de deux murs en angle. Des tables modulaires éclairées par des abat-jour de type industriel permettent de modifier la configuration de la salle facilement. L'harmonisation de l'extérieur a été réalisée à l'aide d'un bardage vertical en sapin.

Der bestehende Verkostungsraum und die Produktionsgebäude sollten ein zeitgemäßes Erscheinungsbild erhalten, welches zwar nach außen hin sichtbar ist, aber nicht in Konflikt mit dem ursprünglichen Charakter der Gebäude tritt. Um die Produktionsabläufe zu vereinfachen, wurde der gesamte Keller um 50 Zentimeter abgesenkt. Weißes, geöltes Holz bestimmt den Charakter des Verkostungsbereichs, dem die breiten Schnittholzdielen und die umlaufende Eckbank zusätzliche Behaglichkeit verleihen. Industrieleuchten und modulare Tischformate ermöglichen Flexibilität. Um das äußere Erscheinungsbild zu vereinheitlichen, wurde ein Großteil der Fassade mit vertikal angeordneten Fichtenhölzern verkleidet.

Architect | Architekten Halbritter & Hillerbrand
Location | Oberer Satzweg 55, 7100 Neusiedl am See, Austria
Year of completion | 2010
Client | Weingut Koppitsch
Type of venue | winery
Type of wine | Blaufränkisch, Weißburgunder, Welschriesling, Neuburger, Zweigelt
Number of seating places | 45
Trained sommelier | yes
Own vineyard | yes
Storage quality | ★★★☆☆

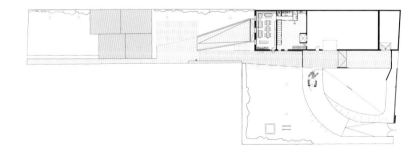

200

WINE & SWEETS TSUMONS
Fukuoka, Japan

This project involved the design for both the shop and bar, providing an original concept to present a new combination of western confectionery and wine. The site is very small and surrounded by multistory apartments. The retail space is located on the side of the building nearest to the road, with the bar to the rear, while the courtyard is situated on the south side. This spatial arrangement gives the bar a quiet atmosphere away from the hustle and bustle on the street outside. The materials used give the design a simple elegance, creating a space that focuses on the products and not on ornamentation.

Les architectes étaient chargés d'élaborer un concept original pour un bar-confiserie devant proposer des produits occidentaux et être construit sur une parcelle très étroite bordée par des immeubles de plusieurs étages. Ils ont positionné la boutique côté rue et le bar du côté de la cour, orientée au sud, de manière à ce que les clients y soient au calme, loin du bruit de la circulation. Les matériaux choisis confèrent aux locaux une sobre élégance, l'accent étant mis plus sur les produits proposés que sur la décoration.

Die Bauaufgabe umfasste die Gestaltung des Verkaufsraumes mit angeschlossener Bar zur Präsentation und zum Verkauf von westlichen Süßwaren und Weinen. Zu diesem Zweck wurde auf einer kleinen Baufläche zwischen mehrstöckigen Appartementhäusern ein neues Gebäude errichtet. Der Verkaufsraum erstreckt sich entlang der Straße, während sich die Bar im hinteren Bereich befindet. Ein Innenhof liegt an der Südseite. Durch diese Anordnung wird der Barbereich vom geschäftigen Treiben auf der Straße abgeschottet. Die verwendeten Materialien verleihen dem Raum eine zurückhaltende Eleganz, in der die präsentierten Produkte ganz im Mittelpunkt stehen können.

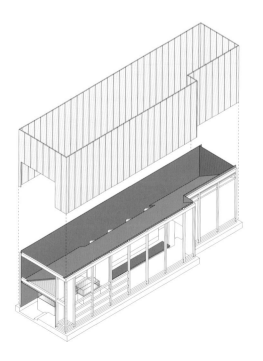

Architect | Case-Real (Koichi Futatsumata, Tomoki Katada)
Location | 1-21-3 Takasago Chuo-Ku, 810-0011 Fukuoka, Japan
Year of completion | 2014
Client | Wine & Sweets Tsumons
Type of venue | retail
Type of wine | dried grape wine, ice wine, botrytized grape wine, flavored wine, fortified wines, champagne, sparkling wine, still wine
Number of seating places | 9
Trained sommelier | yes
Storage quality | ★★★☆☆

WEINGUT & WEINSTUBE KRUGER-RUMPF
Münster-Sarmsheim, Germany

The Kruger-Rumpf winery is a listed building, originally constructed in 1830 and dominated by two opposed buildings. The main building has housed the Kruger-Rumpf winery for more than 15 years and the new extension was intended as an advantageous addition to the complex as a whole. The building work comprised three different tasks: The creation of a new entrance situation, restoration of the listed building, and the demolition and reconstruction of the side wing. The barrel-vaulted room has been cleaned up and now functions as the centerpiece of the entire ensemble. The original staircase now functions as a bar, forming a connecting element between the winery and bar area.

La cave Kruger-Rumpf occupe deux bâtiments classés construits en 1830 qui présentent un aspect on ne peut plus différent. Un bistro servant principalement du vin a été ouvert dans l'un d'eux il y a une quinzaine d'années. La tâche des architectes était triple ici : construction d'un nouveau porche, rénovation du bâtiment en pierre, démolition et reconstruction de l'annexe. La grande salle voûtée, pièce principale de l'ensemble architectural, a retrouvé sa splendeur d'antan. L'ancienne cage d'escalier abrite désormais le comptoir et relie le bistro à l'annexe.

Das denkmalgeschützte Weingut Kruger-Rumpf, erbaut 1830, wird von zwei gegensätzlichen Häusern dominiert. Das Gutshaus beherbergt seit mehr als 15 Jahren die Weinstube Kruger-Rumpf, der Erweiterungsbau kommt der Gesamtanlage zugute. Die Baumaßnahme setzte sich aus drei Aufgaben zusammen: der Neubau des Eingangsbereichs, die Sanierung des denkmalgeschützten Steinhauses und der Abbruch und Wiederaufbau des Seitenflügels. Der tonnengewölbte Raum wurde herausgeputzt und vervollständigt als Herzstück die Anlage. Das ursprüngliche Treppenhaus fungiert heute als Thekenraum und als Bindeglied zwischen Weingut und Weinstube.

Architect | Molter Linnemann Architekten
Location | Rheinstraße 47, 55424 Münster-Sarmsheim,
Germany
Year of completion | 2009
Client | Stephan and Cornelia Rumpf
Type of venue | hospitality
Type of wine | Riesling, Pinot Blanc, Pinot Gris, Pinot
Noir
Own vineyard | yes
Storage quality | ★★★☆☆

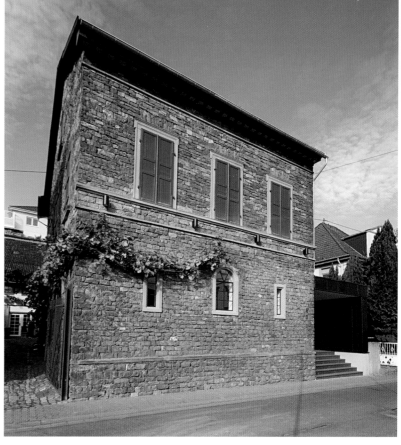

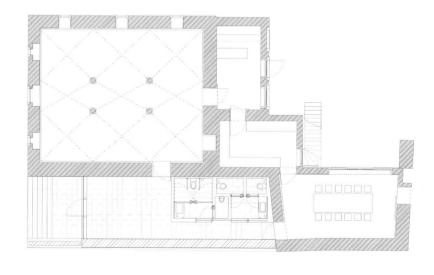

208

Architect | Mattes Riglewski Architekten
Construction Management | Architekturbüro Stoppel
Location | Sonnenbichlstraße 31, 88149 Nonnenhorn, Germany
Year of completion | 2008
Client | Josef and Renate Gierer
Type of venue | retail
Type of wine | white wine, red wine, Müller-Thurgau, Pinot
Number of seating places | tasting only
Own vineyard | yes
Storage quality | ★★★★★

WINZERHOF GIERER
Nonnenhorn, Germany

The Gierer vineyard in Nonnenhorn is located in a raised position just 500 meters from the Lake of Constance. The new sales and tasting areas, together with a barrel cellar, were modernized in order to meet the demands of modern wine production and to improve operations. The new building is a freestanding volume positioned in front of the renovated barn and clearly visible from the entrance driveway. A solid angular wall of Vals quartzite formulates the entrance between the barn and the large tree in the courtyard and structures the sales area into two distinct parts. Upon entering the new tasting area in the old barn, the visitor crosses a glass floor that allows a glimpse into the barrel cellar.

Le chai Gierer est situé à seulement cinq cents mètres de la rive du lac de Constance. Afin d'optimiser la production de vin, il s'est complété récemment d'une annexe abritant un espace de vente/dégustation et une cave à barriques, annexe érigée dans le prolongement d'une grange rénovée. Deux niches, l'une accueillant une banquette, l'autre servant de présentoir pour les différents crus, ont été aménagées dans le mur massif en quartzite de Vals construit entre la grange et le grand catalpa poussant dans la cour. Le sol de l'ancienne grange est partiellement recouvert d'une plaque de verre permettant d'apercevoir les barriques entreposées dans la cave.

Der Winzerhof Gierer in Nonnenhorn liegt etwas erhöht nur 500 Meter vom Bodensee entfernt. Um den Anspruch des Weines gerecht zu werden und die Arbeitsabläufe zu verbessern, wurde ein Neubau errichtet, der den Verkaufs- und Probierraum sowie einen Holzfasskeller beherbergt. Der eigenständige Baukörper vor der renovierten Scheune bildet die sichtbare Adresse des Winzerhofs. Eine massive Wand aus Valser Quarzit formuliert den Eingang zwischen Scheune und dem großen, markanten Hofbaum. Darüber hinaus teilt sie den Verkaufsraum in zwei Bereiche. In die neue Probierstube in der alten Scheune gelangt der Gast über einen gläsernen Fußboden, der ihm einen Blick in den Holzfasskeller ermöglicht.

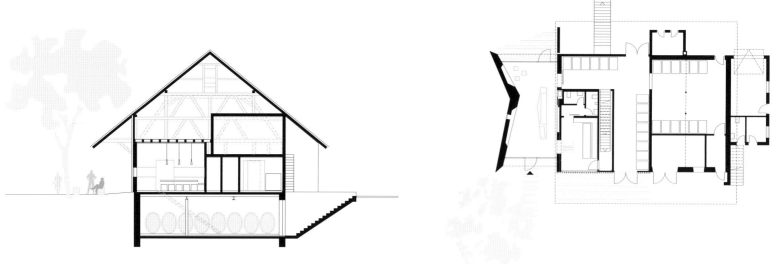

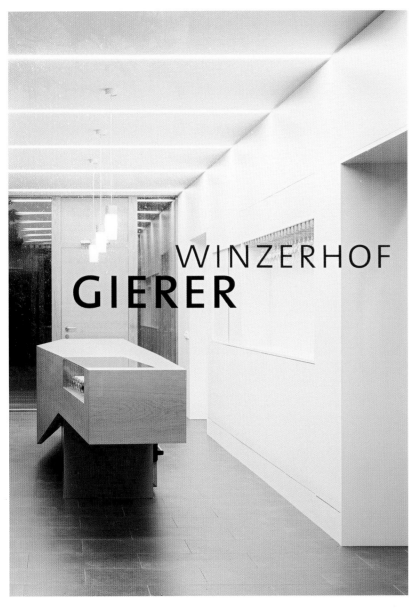

WINZERHOF
GIERER

Architects | Ignacio Urquiza and Bernardo Quinzaños CCA l Centro de Colaboración
Arquitectónica
Location | San Luis de la Paz, Guanajuato, Mexico
Year of completion | 2013
Client | Cuna de Tierra
Type of venue | winery
Type of wine | blends of Cabernet, Nebbiolo, Syrah and Tempranillo
Number of seating places | 40
Cooling and ventilation techniques | natural air cooling and ventilation
Trained sommelier | yes
Own vineyard | yes
Storage quality | ★ ★ ★ ★ ★

VINICOLA CUNA DE TIERRA
Guanajuato, Mexico

The name of the wine Cuna de Tierra (Soil Cradle) served as inspiration for this project. The main material used in the construction was concrete mixed with soil taken from the site. Iron and wood have also been used to strengthen the construction. A number of high-tech systems ensure that the desired amounts of light and air can enter the individual production areas. The design also involved the construction of an observation platform that offers views over the surrounding vineyards. The use of local materials enable the large volume to fit unobtrusively into its surrounding and the wider context.

S'inspirant du nom du vignoble (Cuna de Tierra, c'est-à-dire « berceau en terre »), les architectes ont mélangé de la terre prise sur place au béton utilisé pour construire un bâtiment avec renforts en bois et en acier. Divers dispositifs high-tech garantissent un bon éclairage et une ventilation suffisante des espaces de production en dépit du faible nombre d'ouvertures de l'enveloppe. Le chai proprement dit se complète d'un belvédère offrant une vue panoramique sur le domaine viticole. L'utilisation de matériaux locaux a permis de bien intégrer ce vaste ensemble dans son environnement naturel.

Der Name des produzierten Weines diente als Inspiration für dieses Projekt – Cuna de Tierra (Wiege aus Erde). So wurde als Hauptmaterial ein Gemisch aus Zement und der Erde vor Ort verwendet, während Eisen und Holz als versteifende Konstruktionselemente und für Türen, Durchgänge und Decken dienten. Ein High-Tech-System reguliert Licht-, Luft- und Feuchtigkeitszufuhr, entsprechend den Anforderungen der einzelnen Produktionsschritte zur Weinerzeugung zugeschnitten ist. Der Entwurf beinhaltete auch die Errichtung einer Aussichtsplatform, um Ausblicke über die umliegenden Weinfelder und die neu errichtete Produktionsstätte zu ermöglichen. Durch die Verwendung von lokalen Materialien passen sich die Gebäudekomplexe harmonisch in den Kontext der Landschaft ein.

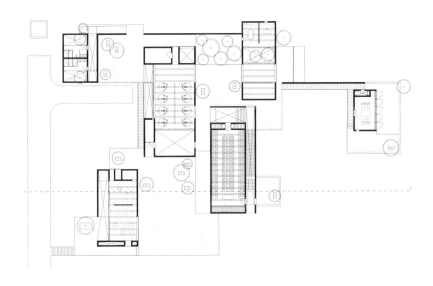

YALUMBA – SIGNATURE CELLAR AND TANKS 11 & 12
Angaston, Australia

Architect | Grieve Gillett
Location | Eden Valley Road, Angaston, Australia
Year of completion | 2011
Client | Yalumba
Type of venue | hospitality
Type of wine | Cabernet Sauvignon & Shiraz, Viognier
Number of seating places | 200
Cooling and ventilation techniques | subterranean
Own vineyard | yes
Storage quality | ★ ★ ★ ★ ☆

Yalumba is Australia's oldest and most successful family owned winery. Grieve Gillett was commissioned to design a dining and wine tasting area for Yalumba's clients and associates. This involved the renovation of the subterranean signature cellar and the conversion of underground concrete wine tanks into private dining and wine tasting rooms. The cellar is fitted with discreet lighting behind new barrel display racks, emphasizing the original rubble walls, achieving a clean, functional open space with richly textured surfaces. The existing wax-sealed concrete tank walls with their wine stained patina were retained. The result is a reflective space disconnected from the outside world, where attention is concentrated on wine, food and conversation.

Le domaine de Yalumba est le plus ancien et le plus réputé des vignobles familiaux d'Australie. Les propriétaires ont récemment chargé Grieve Gillett de rénover la cave et de concevoir un espace de dégustation et une salle de banquet dans les anciennes citernes en béton recouvert de cire patinée par le vin. La salle de banquet est éclairée par des lampes positionnées derrière des barriques et la salle de dégustation par des rampes lumineuses installées sous le sol en planches, cet éclairage indirect ayant l'avantage de mettre en valeur la texture d'origine des murs en béton. Cet espace à l'atmosphère sereine permet aux convives de se concentrer sur le bon vin, la bonne chère et la conversation.

Yalumba ist Australiens ältestes und erfolgreichstes Weingut im Familienbesitz. Grieve Gillett wurde beauftragt, das neue Restaurant und den neuen Verkostungsbereich zu entwerfen. Dies umfasste die Umgestaltung des charakteristischen Weinkellers und den Umbau von ehemaligen Betontanks zu privaten Essens- und Verkostungsräumen. Der Keller wurde mit indirekter Beleuchtung hinter den Lagerregalen der neuen Fässer und zwischen den Holzböden und den Wänden ausgestattet, um die Textur der verputzten historischen Steinmauern und die Patina der mit Wachs versiegelten Mauern der ehemaligen Betontanks zu betonen. Das Ergebnis ist eine besinnliche Atmosphäre, welche die äußere Welt vergessen lässt und Raum für Wein, Essen und Konversation schafft.

221

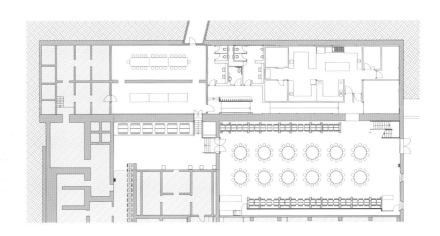

Architect | sistémica
Location | Mariano Escobedo 700, 11590 Mexico City, Mexico
Year of completion | 2014
Client | Intersybarite
Type of venue | retail
Number of seating places | 2
Cooling and ventilation techniques | standard air conditioning
Storage quality | ★★★☆☆

BOUTIQUE INTERSYBARITE
Mexico City, Mexico

This small retail space sells only the best gourmet products. The products take center stage in the design, becoming an eye-catching attraction within a showroom-like setting. This project is the result of a desire to achieve an intriguing and visually striking atmosphere, with the cellar devised as a key element of the design concept. The space is open to the public, stirring the curiosity of passersby and drawing visitors inside. The wood used was recycled from used pallets, which not only gives the design a unique feel, but also helped to reduce cost and environmental impact.

Le design de cette épicerie fine conçue comme un showroom vise à mettre en valeur les produits de qualité proposés à la vente. L'atmosphère séduisante du lieu vient de ce que les architectes ont su tirer le meilleur parti d'une position en sous-sol. L'utilisation exclusive de palettes recyclées pour la décoration intérieure a permis de limiter à la fois les frais de réalisation et l'impact sur l'environnement. Afin d'attirer les clients, la cloison donnant sur la galerie marchande souterraine est entièrement vitrée.

Dieses kleine Geschäft hat sich auf den Verkauf von hochwertigen Gourmetprodukten spezialisiert. Die Produkte bilden den Mittelpunkt des Entwurfs und werden wie in einem Showroom präsentiert. Das Ergebnis ist ein Raum mit einem bestechenden visuellen Konzept, das auf Kelleratmosphäre als zentrales Gestaltungselement basiert. Dafür wurde ausschließlich Holz verwendet, welches von alten Paletten stammt. So entstand nicht nur ein Unikat, sondern auch die Kosten und Auswirkungen auf die Umwelt wurden gering gehalten. Um die Neugier der Passanten auf sich zu ziehen, öffnen sich die Gestaltung und der Raum zur Straßenseite.

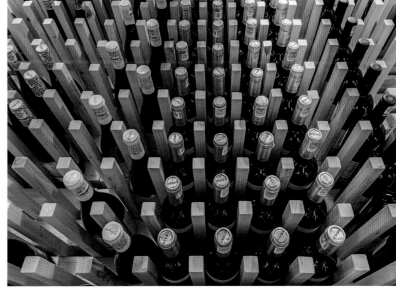

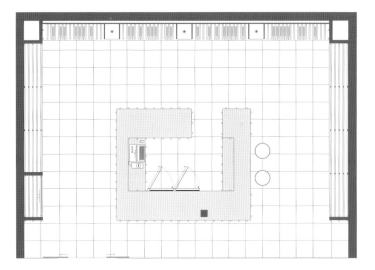

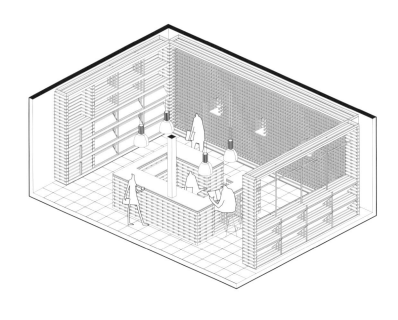

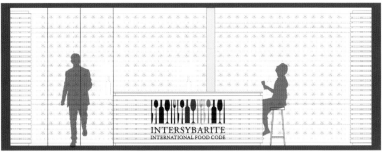

227

BAR LA BOHÈME
(ENTRE AMIS)
Porto, Portugal

Architect | AVA - Atelier Veloso Architects
Location | Rua Galeria de Paris 36/40, 4050-284 Porto, Portugal
Year of completion | 2011
Client | Alberto Nuno Oliveira da Fonseca
Type of venue | hospitality
Number of seating places | approx. 50
Storage quality | ★★★☆☆

The bar La Bohème is located on Rua Galeria de Paris, in the middle of Porto's downtown area. The redesign sought to restructure the space, giving it a new identity. The solution was formalized through the texture and the color of the wood, which defines the space and provides depth to the design. The bar spans three levels: the main floor, basement and a mezzanine. The latter establishes a visual relationship with the main floor. The bar counter is located on the main floor, next to the entrance door and public access. The façade is clad in granite ashlar and all changes made to the façade were solely at the level of framework and entrance span.

Le bar La Bohème se trouve dans la « Rua da Galeria de Paris », l'une des rues du centre ville de Porto. De récents travaux de rénovation ont permis de restructurer l'espace et de renouveler l'image de ce bar sur trois niveaux : rez-de-chaussée, cave et mezzanine. Par sa texture et sa couleur, le bois a contribué à redéfinir l'espace et à lui conférer plus de profondeur. Le comptoir du bar est situé au rez-de-chaussée, près de l'entrée du public. L'intervention sur la façade en granite a uniquement constitué en un élargissement de la porte d'entrée et une modification de la structure des fenêtres.

Die Bar La Bohème befindet sich inmitten von Portos Stadtzentrum in der Rua Galeria de Paris. Die Umgestaltung beinhaltete die Neuordnung des Raumes zur Schaffung einer neuen Identität. Die Architekten nutzten eine Verkleidung aus hellen Hölzern, welche durch ihre Textur und Farbe den Raum strukturiert und ihm Tiefe verleiht. Die Räumlichkeiten erstrecken sich über drei Ebenen: ein Keller, ein Hauptgeschoss auf Straßenebene und ein optisch angebundenes Zwischengeschoss. Die Theke befindet sich im Hauptgeschoss neben dem Eingang. Bei der Gestaltung des Portals wurde bewusst die Verkleidung aus Granitquadern beibehalten und lediglich Änderungen an der Breite des Eingangs und der Struktur der Fenster vorgenommen.

WIJNBAR BALTHAZAR
Sint-Truiden, Belgium

This wine bar is intended as a place where locals can meet and enjoy a lively and comfortable atmosphere. The large display window at the front of the building helps to stir the curiosity of passersby, tempting them inside. A long narrow space joins onto the bar, where people can sit, chat and relax while enjoying a glass of fine wine. The use of authentic materials such as oak and rough-finished surfaces give the bar a rural feel. Wine crates are stacked against the wall, adding a playful element to the design. Steel window frames and industrial lighting at the back of the bar also help to add a vintage twist to the overall appearance.

Ce bar à vin a été conçu afin de permettre à la population locale de se retrouver dans une atmosphère conviviale. Le côté rue entièrement vitré invite les passants à satisfaire leur curiosité en venant voir ce qui se passe à l'intérieur. L'espace tout en longueur qui se trouve près du bar est pourvu de sièges où l'on peut savourer un verre de bon vin entre amis. Des matériaux authentiques, notamment du chêne et des murs en briques recouverts d'un enduit grossier, confèrent à cet espace urbain un caractère rural encore renforcé par les caisses de bouteilles empilées le long des murs. Les fenêtres en acier et les abat-jour industriels donnent par ailleurs au bar un certain côté « vintage ».

Diese Weinbar wurde als Treffpunkt konzipiert, der den Bewohnern des Viertels eine lebendige und komfortable Atmosphäre zum Austausch bietet. Die große Glasfront ermöglicht Einblicke und weckt dadurch die Neugier der Passanten. Ein langgezogener enger Raum schließt sich an die Bar an mit Sitzgelegenheiten für Unterhaltungen bei einem guten Glas Wein. Authentische Materialien wie Eiche und unbehandelte Oberflächen verleihen dem Raum ein ländliches Flair. Gestapelte Weinkisten an den Wänden lockern die Gestaltung auf, während Fensterrahmen aus Stahl und Industrielampen über der Theke dem Gesamtbild einen Vintage-Akzent verleihen.

Designer | Creneau International
Location | Grote Markt 52, 3800 Sint-Truiden, Belgium
Year of completion | 2012
Client | Maurice Vroonen
Type of venue | hospitality
Number of seating places | approx. 50
Trained sommelier | yes
Storage quality | ★★★★☆

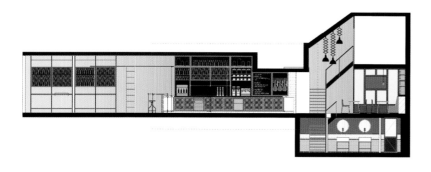

234

Architect | robanus architekten
Location | Sonnenbichlstraße 8, 88149 Nonnenhorn, Germany
Year of completion | 2012
Client | Lanz.Wein
Type of venue | retail
Type of wine | Johanniter, Cabernet Blanc, Solaris, Cabertin, Pinotin
Number of seating places | 30
Cooling and ventilation techniques | natural cooling
Own vineyard | yes
Storage quality | ★★★★★

LANZ.WEIN
Nonnenhorn, Germany

This project involved the extension of the existing building to include a tasting room, wine storage space and cellar. A two-story steel construction was built in order to accommodate the new rooms. The newly designed façade facing the street is characterized by its smooth surface, which clearly differentiates it from the existing building. Large glazed sections offer passersby views into the tasting room and wine cellar: Here, a rammed-earth wall has been used to establish a connection between the design and the vineyard. The wall niches also serve as showcases for the wine. The use of natural materials such as clay, wood, glass and stone responds to the company's ecological philosophy.

L'utilisation de poutres en acier a permis de réaménager ce bâtiment viticole en optimisant l'espace, de sorte qu'on y trouve aujourd'hui une salle de dégustation, un espace de stockage et une cave. La façade sur rue se distingue non seulement par son enduit lisse, mais aussi par ses larges surfaces vitrées qui permettent d'apercevoir le mur en torchis réalisé avec de la terre locale, mur dans lequel on a aménagé des niches servant de présentoirs à bouteilles. Outre le torchis, l'architecte a également privilégié des matériaux naturels tels que le bois, la pierre et le verre de manière à respecter les convictions écologiques des propriétaires.

Das bestehende Wirtschaftsgebäude wurde um Probierstube, Weinlager und Kellereibereiche ergänzt, die durch den Einbau einer Stahlkonstruktion platzsparend auf zwei Ebenen untergebracht werden konnten. Die neugestaltete Fassade zur Straße hebt sich durch ihre glatte Oberfläche deutlich von der bestehenden Fassade ab. Große Verglasungen erlauben Passanten Einblicke in Weinkeller und Probierstube, die durch eine Stampflehmwand aus der Bodensubstanz des Weinbergs eine besondere Raumatmosphäre erhielt. In die Wand eingelassene Nischen dienen als Ausstellungsvitrinen für die Weine. Der Einsatz von Lehm rundet die Auswahl natürlicher Materialien wie Holz, Glas und Stein entsprechend der ökologischen Philosophie des Betriebs ab.

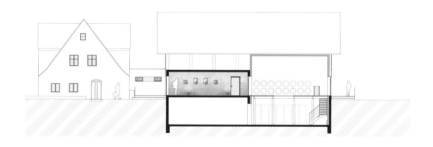

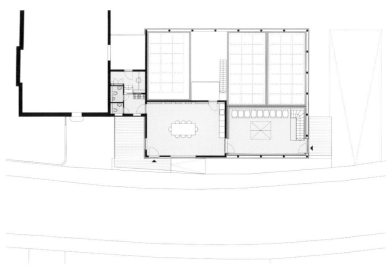

BVS WINE TRADERS
Bucharest, Romania

The main idea behind this design was to create a wine library, capable of displaying as many bottles as possible and using their labels, colors and shapes as the main elements in the space, while simultaneously offering a tasting room for the clients to uncork and taste the wines before buying. The goal was to create a postindustrial look, combining 'natural' materials and colors such as local plywood, stone and steel, with recycled elements recovered from the existing building such as brick walls and wooden beams, in order to create an intimate atmosphere for wine tasting.

L'idée de base pour cette vinothèque était double : exposer le plus grand nombre possible de bouteilles en utilisant la couleur et la forme des étiquettes comme des éléments décoratifs, et créer une salle de dégustation où les clients pourraient déboucher le vin et le goûter avant de l'acheter. Avec pour résultat un bâtiment de style postindustriel qui « recycle » les briques et les poutres d'origine et associe des matériaux naturels tels que le carton, la pierre et l'acier de manière à générer une atmosphère conviviale pour les amateurs de bon vin.

Hauptidee des Entwurfs war eine Weinbibliothek zu kreieren, welche zahlreiche Weine präsentieren kann und die Etiketten, Farben und Formen als Gestaltungsmittel nutzt. Gleichzeitig wird die Möglichkeit zur Verkostung angeboten, werden Weine vor dem Kauf entkorkt und probiert. Ein postindustrielles Ambiente, in dem natürliche Materialien und Farben wie Sperrholz, Stein und Stahl mit Elementen des bestehenden Gebäudes wie Backsteinmauer und Holzbalken kombiniert werden, war Ziel des Entwurf für die Weinverkostung in intimer Atmosphäre.

Architect | beros & abdul architects
Location | Strada Covaci 19, 030094 Bucharest,
Romania
Year of completion | 2012
Client | BvS Wine Traders
Type of venue | retail
Type of wine | worldwide
Number of seating places | 20
Storage quality | ★★★☆☆

242

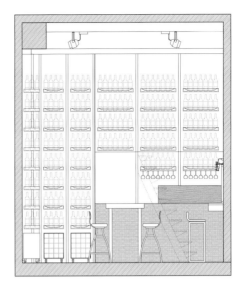

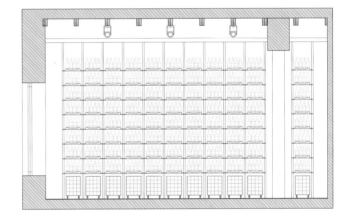

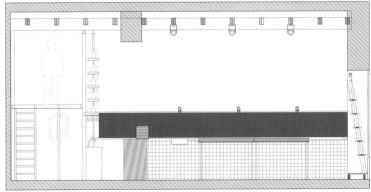

Architect | stereoraum Architekten
Lighting | Andreas Becker
Location | Schneiderstraße 2, 55596 Waldböckelheim, Germany
Year of completion | 2012
Client | Weingut Funck-Schowalter
Type of venue | winery, retail
Type of wine | Riesling, Pinot Blanc, Pinot Noir and Pinot Gris
Number of seating places | 9
Own vineyard | yes
Storage quality | ★★★☆☆

VINOTHEK FUNCK-SCHOWALTER
Waldböckelheim, Germany

Thomas Funck wanted to find a new approach to presenting and selling wine. Integrated into the existing courtyard structure, this cubic structure is well suited to the surrounding context and, in terms of both form and structure, is reminiscent of the stonewalls that can be found along the foot of the Kirchberg. The exterior walls have a broom finish. Even the fittings and furnishings of this vinotheque are designed to set the perfect stage to present the high-quality wines on offer. The bottles of premium wines are presented at eye level in a gallery of white-gold display units. Rough plaster has been used inside, combined with warm tones and colors that create a welcoming atmosphere. In summer, wine tasting takes place on the outdoor terrace.

Le propriétaire de ce chai souhaitait disposer d'un nouveau bâtiment pour présenter sa production sous un jour différent. Les architectes ont intégré au bâti préexistant un volume dont la forme et la structure rappellent les murets en pierre de la colline voisine de Kirchberg. Les murs de ce bâtiment sont recouverts d'un enduit « au balai » — une technique traditionnelle remise au goût du jour à cette occasion. Le mobilier et l'éclairage de la vinothèque ont été spécialement conçus pour mettre en valeur la production du domaine, les crus haut de gamme étant présentés individuellement sur des colonnettes blanches et dorées. La structure brute de l'enduit extérieur se retrouve à l'intérieur, la teinte chaude du revêtement rappelant la couleur du sol du terroir. En été, il est possible de déguster le vin sur la terrasse.

Neue Wege wollte Thomas Funck gehen und seinen Weinen einen passenden Rahmen zur Präsentation geben. Eingebunden in die bereits bestehende Hofstruktur passt sich der Kubus an die Umgebung an und erinnert in Form und Struktur an die Bruchsteinmauern am Fuße des Kirchbergs. Für die Außenwände wurde eine alte Putztechnik, der Besenstrich, wiederbelebt. Die Vinothek ist bis hin zur Möblierung und Lichtplanung ganz auf die Inszenierung der edlen Weine ausgerichtet. Die Premiumweine präsentieren sich auf Augenhöhe in einer Galerie auf weiß-goldenen Stelen. Auch im Innenraum wurde eine raue Putzstruktur gewählt, die Farbgebung ist warm und erinnert an das Terroir der Weine. Im Sommer findet die Weinprobe auf der Terrasse statt.

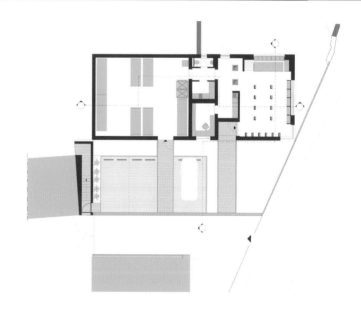

247

Architect | Kreatif Architects
Location | Kuscuburun Mahallesi, Yazibasi Beldesi 4, Torbali, Turkey
Year of completion | 2014
Client | LA Wines
Type of venue | winery
Type of wine | Tempranillo, Chenin Blanc, Viognier, Marselan, Trebbiano, Ugni Blanc, Cabernet Sauvignon, Merlot, Chardonnay, Misket types of wines
Number of seating places | 200
Cooling and ventilation techniques | VRF outdoor conditioning units
Trained sommelier | yes
Own vineyard | yes
Storage quality | ★★★★★

248

LA WINERY
Torbali, Turkey

The LA vineyards are oriented north-south, with the main building located to the north-west of the site. The building houses two main functions: a wine tasting area and the cellar. The wine tasting space demanded a welcoming atmosphere with sunlight, natural ventilation and an orientation toward the vista, whereas the cellar requires a controlled climate and a dim atmosphere. Wide glass windows in the tasting area provide visual contact with the cellar space beneath. The 3,000-square-meter underground cellar consists of curvilinear raw concrete surfaces that were cast with steel molds. Additionally, this space also includes a special wine tasting space that is open to the vista via the lower level.

Le chai se trouve au nord-ouest de ce vignoble dont les vignes sont orientées nord-sud. La salle de dégustation bénéficie d'une ventilation et d'un éclairage naturels et offre une vue superbe sur le paysage, ce qui contribue à la rendre particulièrement accueillante. Le bâtiment est construit sur une cave de trois mille mètres carrés qui permet de stocker le vin dans des conditions idéales. Des dalles en verre installées dans la salle de dégustation permettent d'apercevoir cette remarquable cave voûtée en béton brut de coffrage, dans laquelle se trouve un second espace de dégustation. On notera que le coffrage a été réalisé avec des plaques d'acier.

Die Weinfelder des LA Weinguts sind in Nord-Süd Richtung ausgerichtet; das Hauptgebäude liegt an der Nord-West-Seite des Geländes. Der Verkostungsbereich des Gebäudes wurde durch die Zufuhr von Frischluft und Sonnenlicht und den Ausblick über das Weingut besonders einladend gestaltet, während der Weinkeller ein optimales und kontrollierbares Klima zur Lagerung der Weine bietet. Große Glasfenster im Boden des Verkostungsbereichs ermöglichen Einblicke in den 3.000 Quadratmeter umfassenden Keller, dessen gewölbte Oberflächen aus unbehandeltem Sichtbeton mit Stahlschalungselementen gegossen wurden. Darüber hinaus bietet er einen durch eine Glaswand abgetrennten Raum zur Weinprobe.

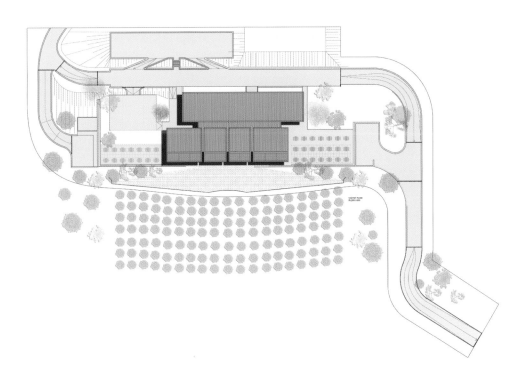

SOKOL BLOSSER WINERY
Dayton, OR, USA

In 2012, Sokol Blosser Winery commissioned Allied Works to develop a master plan and design a new tasting room and event space for the estate. The Sokol Blosser family has been producing Pinot noir, Pinot gris and other varieties since 1977. The new building provides a range of spaces for sampling the family's wines and viewing their estate in Oregon's Dundee Hills. At the center of the building is a main tasting room featuring a bar, outdoor terrace, sitting area and hearth with spectacular views of the Yamhill Valley. A library and kitchen flank the tasting room and offer a range of scales and spatial qualities for gathering and wine tasting. A new cellar is embedded in the earth, providing space for private tastings and wine storage.

Le chai Sokol Blosser, situé en Oregon dans les Dundee Hills, produit depuis 1977 du vin à base de divers cépages, notamment du pinot noir et gris. En 2012, les propriétaires ont demandé au bureau d'architectes Allied Works de concevoir une annexe devant abriter une salle de dégustation et un espace événementiel avec vue sur le domaine. La salle de dégustation, située au centre du nouveau bâtiment et flanquée d'une bibliothèque et d'une cuisine, inclut un bar et se prolonge par une terrasse donnant sur la vallée de Yamhill. L'espace est modulable de manière à pouvoir accueillir des événements œnologiques rassemblant un public plus ou moins nombreux. L'ensemble se complète d'une véritable cave permettant de stocker le vin dans des conditions adéquates.

2012 beauftragte das Weingut Sokol Blosser Allied Works ein Gestaltungskonzept für einen neuen Verkostungs- und Eventraum zu entwickeln. Die Räumlichkeiten sollten zahlreiche Möglichkeiten zur Präsentation der produzierten Weine bieten und gleichzeitig Ausblicke über das Anwesen der Familie in Yamhill County ermöglichen. Das Zentrum des Gebäudes ist der Hauptverkostungsraum mit Bar, Terrasse, Sitzbereich und fantastischen Ausblicken über das Yamhill Valley, flankiert von einer Bibliothek und der Küche. Zusammen ergeben sich so flexible Raumaufteilungen für unterschiedlich große Veranstaltungen. Darüber hinaus wurde ein neuer Weinkeller entworfen, der neben der Weinlagerung Platz für private Weinproben bietet.

Architect | Allied Works Architecture
Location | 5000 Sokol Blosser Lane, 97114 Dayton,
OR, USA
Year of completion | 2013
Client | Sokol Blosser Winery
Type of venue | winery
Type of wine | Pinot Noir, Pinot Gris
Number of seating places | 51
Cooling and ventilation techniques | in-ground cellar,
passive shading
Trained sommelier | yes
Own vineyard | yes
Storage quality | ★★★★★

LA GALERIE DU VIN
Zurich, Switzerland

La Galerie du Vin serves as both sales, tasting and seminar space that appeals to both customers and passersby alike. The design concept by OOS responds to the company's values and traditions, placing the wine itself at the center of the design. The walls are covered with around 1,500 wine crates from the Bordeaux region, giving the space an almost grotto-like character. Organized into a platform, these crates accommodate approximately 570 wine bottles, as well as serving as illuminated tables and seating elements. A reception counter is located in the center of the room; its violet and ruby colors create a striking contrast to the light wood of the wine crates.

À la fois espace de vente, lieu de dégustation et salle de conférences, la Galerie du Vin a ses habitués et sait attirer de nouveaux clients. Il s'agit d'une entreprise traditionnelle réaménagée par le bureau d'architectes OOS afin de mettre le vin en valeur. Les quelques 1500 caisses de bouteilles accrochées au plafond et empilées le long des murs de manière irrégulière confèrent à cet espace l'aspect d'une grotte — et servent accessoirement d'étagères, de sièges et de présentoirs pour les 570 sortes de vin proposées à la vente. Le comptoir, seul élément de couleur dans cet intérieur dominé par le bois brut, est d'une teinte adéquate : lie-de-vin.

La Galerie du Vin ist sowohl Verkaufs- als auch Degustations- und Seminarraum und vermag Stammkunden und Passanten gleichermaßen anzusprechen. Das Raumkonzept von OOS greift die Werte und Traditionen des Unternehmens auf und stellt die Weinflaschen in den Mittelpunkt. Etwa 1.500 Weinkisten aus der Region von Bordeaux bedecken den gesamten Raum bis hin zur Decke und bilden eine grottenähnliche Umgebung. In einem Raster angeordnet dienen sie als Podestfläche für rund 570 Weine, beleuchtete Tischvitrinen sowie Bücher und Sitzflächen. Der als Theke dienende Empfang in der Mitte des Raumes ist für die Weinberatung ausgestattet und kontrastiert mit seinem violett/rubinfarbenen Ton mit dem Holz der Weinkisten.

Architect | OOS
Location | Feldstrasse 62, 8004 Zurich, Switzerland
Year of completion | 2010
Client | Albert Reichmuth
Type of venue | retail
Type of wine | European wines
Number of seating places | 8
Own vineyard | yes
Storage quality | ★★★☆☆

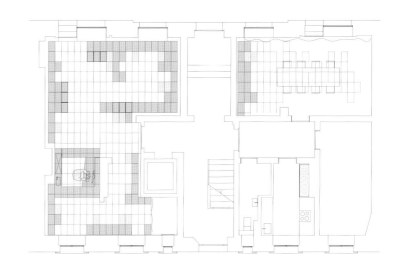

TORKEL LEVANTI
Fläsch, Switzerland

Levanti is a small but dignified wine producer located in Fläsch, Switzerland. The design concept for this project involved adding an apartment to the original wine pressing area. The original appearance of the building has been maintained, although a cellar was added underground in order to provide additional workspace. The arched entrance reveals the double function of the space: A recessed glazed sliding door leads into the tasting area, adjacent to the apartment entrance. The entire design is characterized by the use of steel and rammed earth.

Levanti est un petit producteur de vin suisse haut de gamme implanté dans le vignoble de Fläsch. Les architectes étaient ici chargés de réaménager un ancien pressoir et de le compléter par un appartement. Tout en respectant le bâti d'origine, ils ont creusé une cave qui agrandit l'espace affecté à la vinification. Un porche dans œuvre aménagé derrière une grande porte voûtée met en évidence la double fonction du bâtiment, puisqu'il donne accès d'un côté à l'appartement, de l'autre à la salle de dégustation vitrée. L'acier brut et le béton compacté sont les deux principaux matériaux utilisés durant les travaux de rénovation.

Levanti ist eine kleine, aber hochwertige Weinmanufaktur in Fläsch. Die Neugestaltung sah die Erweiterung der in einem alten Torkelgebäude gelegenen Räumlichkeiten um eine Wohnung vor. Dabei blieb die Bausubstanz der historischen Gebäudehülle unangetastet, während ein Arbeitsraum unterkellert wurde, um zusätzlichen Platz für den Weinbaubetrieb zu schaffen. Der Eingang im Torbogen verrät bereits die neue Doppelnutzung: Die zurückversetzte, verglaste Schiebefront des Verkostungsbereichs wurde durch den Eingang zur Wohnung ergänzt. Für den Umbau wurden hauptsächlich roher Stahl und Stampfbeton verwendet.

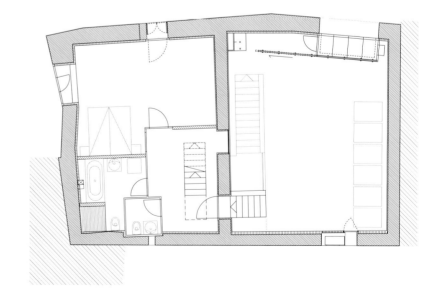

Architect | atelier-f architekten
Location | Bovelweg 29, 7306 Fläsch, Switzerland
Year of completion | 2013
Client | Walter and Elly Süsstrunk
Type of venue | winery
Type of wine | Pinot Noir
Number of seating places | 20
Own vineyard | yes
Storage quality | ★★★☆☆

264

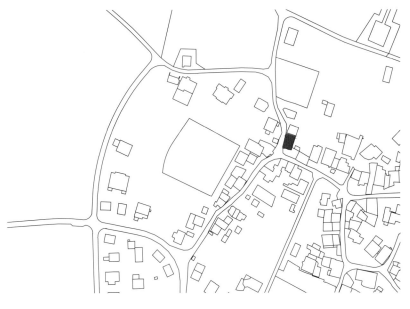

Architect | Michael Egger Aix Architects
Location | Lennacher Straße 7, 74189 Weinsberg-Gellmersbach, Germany
Year of completion | 2011
Client | Wolf Peter Leiss
Type of venue | winery
Type of wine | Trollinger, Lemberger, Riesling, Pinot gris, Pinot noir
Number of seating places | 90
Own vineyard | yes
Storage quality | ★★★★☆

266

WEINGUT LEISS
Weinsberg-Gellmersbach, Germany

The extension of this traditional family vineyard respects the surrounding landscape and existing buildings. The new design seeks to establish a sense of continuity and a careful symbiosis of old and new. The two-story connecting building is characterized by the large glass entrance that refines the light tones of the wood and the fine structures of the fixtures and fittings. A showroom is located below the tasting area and welcomes visitors with built-in display cases and a wide bar. A connecting corridor leads out onto the terrace, from where guests can enjoy sweeping views of the landscape. The retail and bar areas boast a rear wall of regional sandstone panels.

Cette annexe construite pour une exploitation viticole familiale de type traditionnel est d'un style en harmonie avec le bâti préexistant et l'environnement naturel. Elle s'inscrit dans la continuité en établissant une synthèse subtile entre l'ancien et le moderne. Dans le nouveau bâtiment sur deux niveaux, une façade entièrement vitrée met en valeur le mobilier finement structuré et un revêtement mural en bois clair. Au niveau inférieur se trouvent un mur-vitrine et un large comptoir. De plus, une grande terrasse permet d'apprécier une vue remarquable sur le paysage. Notons pour terminer que le mur principal de l'espace de vente et de dégustation est recouvert d'un parement en plaques de grès d'origine locale.

Der Ausbau des traditionellen Weinguts der Familie Leiss respektiert Landschaft und Bestand in hohem Maße. Die gesamte Neugestaltung ist auf Kontinuität und eine sorgsame Symbiose von Alt und Neu bedacht. Der neue zweigeschossige Verbindungsbau veredelt den hellen Holzton und die feine Struktur der Einbauten durch eine großzügige Glasfront. Darunter empfängt ein Schauraum mit eingebauter Wandvitrine und breitem Präsentationspult die Besucher. Ein breiter Verbindungsraum führt auf eine große Terrasse hinaus, die den Blick auf die Landschaft frei gibt. Die Rückwand des gesamten Verkaufs- und Ausschankbereichs besteht aus regionalen Sandsteinplatten.

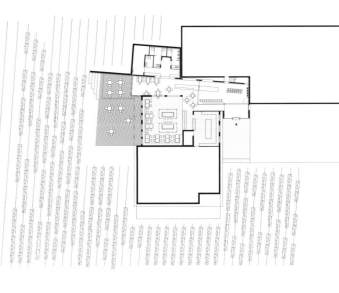

Architect | Architekten Halbritter & Hillerbrand
Location | Augasse 11, 7163 Andau, Austria
Year of completion | 2013
Client | Weingut Reeh
Type of venue | winery
Type of wine | Zweigelt, Merlot, Chardonnay, Sauvignon Blanc
Number of seating places | 20
Cooling and ventilation techniques | heat exchangers for heating and cooling
Own vineyard | yes
Storage quality | ★★★★☆

WEINGUT REEH
Andau, Austria

This new winery, owned by Hannes Reeh, is located on the outskirts of Andau. Designed as a traditional winery, the production, storage, sales and tasting areas all come together to form a unified building ensemble. A key focus of the design was the creation of a wine 'stage' that operates as a platform for all those involved in the process of winemaking and selling. The design is timeless and flexible and the facilities can easily be expanded in the future. The design of the production area was planned in accordance with the processes that take place: The wine press, bottling area, and vat room are at the core of the design, adjacent to the public spaces, sales and tasting areas.

Le nouveau chai construit à la demande de Hannes Reeh est situé à la périphérie du village d'Andau. Fidèle à la tradition viticole locale, il rassemble sous un même toit les espaces de production, de stockage, de dégustation et de vente. L'idée de base était de construire une « scène pour le vin », c'est-à-dire une plate-forme ouverte à tous les acteurs de la vinification. Les architectes ont opté pour un style flexible et intemporel de manière à ce que le bâtiment puisse être agrandi à l'avenir sans problème. L'espace est structuré en fonction des différentes étapes de production : pressoir, élevage du vin, mise en bouteille, dégustation et vente.

Am Ortsrand von Andau befindet sich das neue Weingut von Hannes Reeh. Im Stil eines traditionellen Winzerbetriebs entworfen, bilden die Räumlichkeiten für Produktion, Lagerung, Verkauf und Verkostung ein geschlossenes Gebäudeensemble. Grundgedanke des Entwurfs war die Schaffung einer ‚Bühne des Weines', welche als Plattform für alle beteiligten Akteure dienen soll. Die Gestaltung wurde bewusst zeitlos und flexibel gehalten, um eine Erweiterung in der Zukunft zu ermöglichen. Die Produktionsbereiche wurden in Abstimmung auf die Arbeitsabläufe geplant, wobei der Press- und Abfüllraum mit dem Tankraum den Kern bildet, an dem öffentliche Bereiche, Verkaufs- und Verkostungsraum angrenzen.

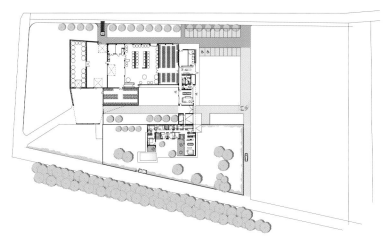

Architect | geis & brantner
Location | Badbergstraße 44, 79235 Vogtsburg-Oberbergen, Germany
Year of completion | 2013
Client | Weingut Franz Keller, Schwarzer Adler
Type of venue | winery
Type of wine | Pinot Gris, Pinot Blanc, Müller-Thurgau, Chardonnay, Riesling,
Silvaner, Sauvignon Blanc, Gewürztraminer, Pinot Noir, Merlot, Cabernet Sauvignon
Number of seating places | max. 250
Cooling and ventilation techniques | natural thermal cooling, optimized cooling circuit
Trained sommelier | yes
Own vineyard | yes
Storage quality | ★★★☆☆

274

WEINGUT KELLER
Vogtsburg-Oberbergen, Germany

The design for this new winery concentrates on fusing architecture and nature and making the most of gravity to aid the winemaking process. In keeping with the terraces carved into the Kaiserstuhl mountain range, the new building is closely connected to the landscape. The design concept divides the winery into three levels, giving the building a harmonious character. The green roofs have been sown with a mixture of meadow seeds from the local area. The wine production area is in use for just two months of the year and is used as a multipurpose event space throughout the rest of the year.

Ce chai entièrement nouveau répond à deux principes directeurs : intégration des bâtiments dans l'environnement naturel et utilisation optimale de la pesanteur pour les diverses étapes de vinification. De fait, ces bâtiments sur trois niveaux partiellement enterrés sont en parfaite harmonie avec les terrasses viticoles taillées dans le massif du Kaiserstuhl. Les toits plats ont été végétalisés avec une variété d'herbe locale. Les locaux destinés à la production du vin n'étant utilisés qu'environ deux mois par an, ils sont convertibles en une salle polyvalente pouvant accueillir des événements durant le reste de l'année.

Entscheidende Grundlage des Entwurfs zum Neubau des Weinguts war das Verschmelzen von Gebäude und Natur bei optimaler Nutzung der Gravitation für die Weinbereitung. Entsprechend der Terrassen des Kaiserstuhls verbindet sich das Gebäude mit der Landschaft. Durch die Aufteilung in drei Ebenen scheint es mit der Umgebung zu verschmelzen. Sämtliche Dachflächen sind mit Wiesensaatgut vom benachbarten Badberg begrünt. Die Produktionsflächen, welche lediglich für etwa zwei Monate im Jahr zur Weinbereitung benötigt werden, werden in der verbleibenden Zeit als multifunktionelle Veranstaltungsflächen genutzt.

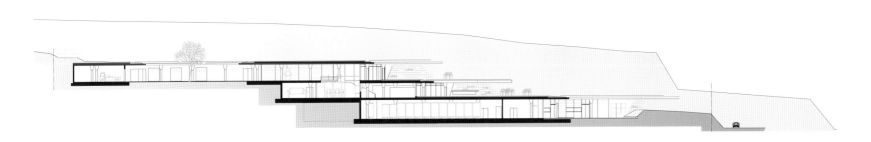

Architect | MoDus Architects
Artist | Manfred Alois Mayr
Location | 39057 Appiano, Italy
Year of completion | 2009
Client | Margareth and Hans Terzer
Type of venue | private wine cellar
Number of seating places | 16
Own vineyard | yes
 Storage quality | ★★★★★

280

HOUSE TERZER
Appiano, Italy

Located in a uniquely South-Tyrolean landscape this house zigzags across a narrow, elongated plot of land, keeping low to the ground to offer but a glimpse of the traditionally tiled roof to those passing by. During the initial excavation work an enormous porphyry boulder was found exactly where the wine cellar and water court were to be located in the lower levels. The water garden is carved into the highest point of the boulder whose jagged profile is then found running into the wine tasting room and wine cellar. A large copper spout dips down from the cantilevered roof of the master bedroom to direct the rainwater into the cavernous water garden below.

Cette maison de vigneron au plan en zigzag a été construite sur un terrain tout en longueur situé dans un site magnifique du Haut-Adige. Afin de favoriser son intégration à l'environnement, elle ne s'élève que légèrement au-dessus du sol en pente et est couverte d'un toit traditionnel en shingles. Les travaux de décaissement ont mis au jour un gigantesque bloc de porphyre juste à l'endroit où la cave devait être creusée. Laissé sur place, ce bloc de roche constitue désormais l'un des murs de la cave/salle de dégustation. Les bassins qui y ont été creusés sur la face supérieure sont alimentés par l'eau de pluie se déversant du toit en surplomb par une gargouille en cuivre.

Inmitten der einzigartigen Landschaft Südtirols gelegen, wurde das Gebäude auf einem länglichen Grundstück errichtet. Der zick-zack-förmige Aufbau wurde dabei bewusst niedrig gehalten, sodass von Weitem gerade mal das traditionelle Schindeldach sichtbar ist. Während der Aushubarbeiten wurde ein gigantischer Porphyryfelsen an der Stelle des geplanten Weinkellers und Wasserhofs freigelegt. Der Wassergarten wurde in die Oberseite des Felsblocks gehauen, dessen zerklüftete Oberfläche sich als Wand im Verkostungsraum und Weinkeller fortsetzt. Um das Regenwasser in den höhlenartigen Wassergarten zu leiten, erhielt das auskragende Dach einen großen Wasserspeier aus Kupfer.

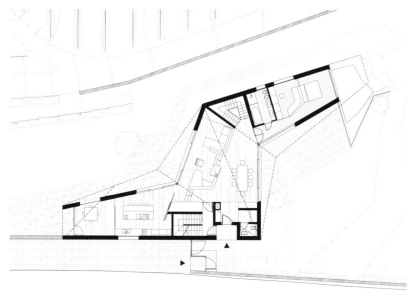

A SHRINE FOR WINE
Istanbul, Turkey

Architect | Focus Wine Cellars
Location | Sarıyer, İstanbul, Turkey
Year of completion | 2007
Client | confidential
Type of venue | private wine cellar
Type of wine | Mediterranean wines
Cooling and ventilation techniques | Fondis purpose-built wine cellar air-conditioners
Storage quality | ★★★★☆

This private cellar has a unique design that radiates a fantastical feeling of space. The wine bottles are arranged on CNC-cut glass shelves in a polar array of 300 degrees from the ceiling to the floor. This ultra-modern setting, combined with ingeniously concealed LED illumination, gives the interior of the wine cellar a striking quality. From the outside, the cellar is a curious illuminated cylinder at the back of the living area. Profound detailing and exquisite workmanship ensure the maintenance of the ideal climate conditions inside. The cellar exemplifies Focus Wine Cellar's ability to combine style with technical perfectionism.

Cette cave à vin privée gère l'espace de manière parfaitement exceptionnelle. Un éclairage par diodes habilement masquées vient renforcer l'impression de modernité qui s'en dégage. La cave proprement dite est un grand cylindre illuminé installé au fond d'un vaste salon. Des étagères à bouteilles, en verre découpé avec une machine CNC pour former des couronnes de cercle à 300 degrés, s'y échelonnent sur toute la hauteur des murs. Divers équipements sophistiqués, alliés à une excellente finition, garantissent des conditions climatiques optimales. Cette réalisation souligne l'expertise de la société Focus Wine Cellars en matière de cave à vin.

Das Konzept dieses privaten Weinkellers vermittelt ein einmaliges Raumgefühl. Die Flaschen sind auf CNC-gefrästen Glasregalen angeordnet, welche den Raum vom Boden bis zur Decke in einem Radius von 300° füllen. Zusammen mit der versteckten LED-Beleuchtung ergibt sich ein beeindruckendes, hochmodernes Erscheinungsbild. Von außen betrachtet erscheint der Weinkeller als erleuchteter Zylinder am Ende des Wohnbereichs, während ausgeklügelte Details und perfektes Handwerk im Inneren ideale klimatische Bedingungen ermöglichen. Dieses Projekt steht beispielhaft für Focus Wine Cellar's Fähigkeit, Design mit technischer Präzision zu verbinden.

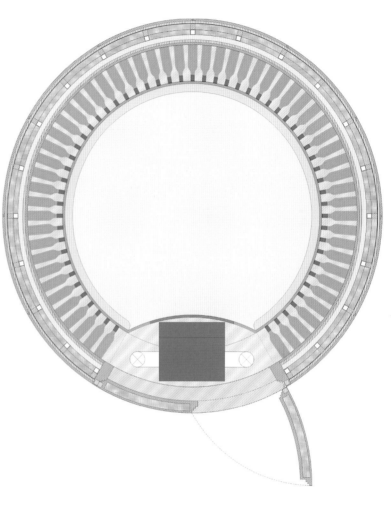

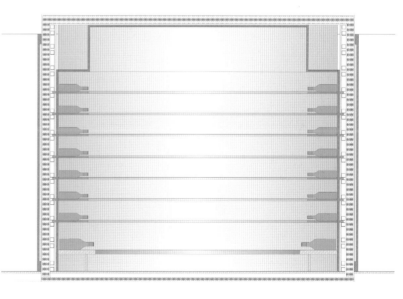

Architect | Christian de Portzamparc
Location | Château Cheval Blanc, 33330 Saint-Émilion, France
Year of completion | 2011
Client | Château Cheval Blanc
Type of venue | winery
Type of wine | Cabernet Franc, Merlot
Cooling and ventilation techniques | heat pump
Own vineyard | yes
Storage quality | ★★★★★

288

CHÂTEAU CHEVAL BLANC
Saint-Émilion, France

Christian de Portzamparc was asked to design a new winery, with a view to improving wine production at Château Cheval Blanc. He envisioned a winery shaped like a belvedere, projecting out from the château and opening onto the beautiful landscape. In this striking design no line is superfluous, everything contributes to perfecting the winemaking process: The geometry of the curved surfaces in molded concrete, the concrete vats shaped like a tasting glass to optimize oxygenation and the unique atmosphere created by the natural light descending earthwards, caressing the load-bearing shear wall. The barrel winery below is like a crypt and has a totally different atmosphere, bordered by a brick moucharaby wall to facilitate natural ventilation.

Les propriétaires du château Cheval Blanc ont demandé à Christian de Portzamparc de réaliser un nouveau chai permettant d'améliorer les différents processus de vinification. L'architecte l'a conçu comme un promontoire/belvédère implanté dans le prolongement du bâti préexistant, d'où l'on découvre la beauté du paysage. Aucune ligne n'est superflue et tout participe à l'optimisation de la production, qu'il s'agisse des surfaces courbes en béton moulé, des cuves en forme de verres garantissant une oxygénation optimale, ou encore de la lumière naturelle qui descend vers le sol en caressant les murs porteurs. Le chai à barriques installé au sous-sol, comme dans une crypte, présente des murs en briques ajourées assurant une bonne ventilation naturelle.

Das Weingut Château Cheval Blanc beauftragte Christian de Portzamparc mit dem Entwurf eines neuen Gebäudes zur Weinproduktion. Der Bau erstreckt sich einer Aussichtsterrasse gleich aus dem Schloss heraus in die Landschaft. Jedes Detail dient der Optimierung der Weinherstellung: Von der Geometrie der geschwungenen Linien des Baukörpers aus Gussbeton, über die Betonfässer in Form von Weingläsern, welche eine optimale Belüftung erlaubt, bis hin zu dem Spiel des Lichts, das sich auf den tragenden Wänden abzeichnet. Der an eine Krypta erinnernde Fasskeller hat eine komplett andere Atmosphäre. Seine Wände aus durchbrochenem Ziegelmauerwerk erleichtern die Belüftung.

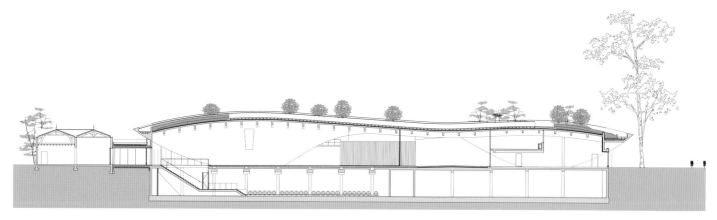

STATE-OF-THE-ART WINE CELLAR
Istanbul, Turkey

Architect | Focus Wine Cellars
Location | Beylerbeyi, İstanbul, Turkey
Year of completion | 2012
Client | confidential
Type of venue | private wine cellar
Type of wine | mainly old world wines
Number of seating places | 6
Cooling and ventilation techniques | Fondis purpose-built wine cellar air-conditioners
Storage quality | ★ ★ ★ ★ ★

This project is characterized by its passionate and intelligent design and a production process that involved intensive craftsmanship at every stage. Arranged around the domed dining area, a U-shaped wine cellar houses 2,000 bottles of rare and fine wines. All lighting, air conditioning and music systems are controlled through a tablet computer that also includes a sophisticated wine management system. The settings in this state-of-the-art wine cellar can be monitored and adjusted by remote. This cellar is a magnificent blend of sophisticated design, finest workmanship, materials and high-tech installations.

Cette cave privée se caractérise par un design intelligent et le soin apporté à la sélection et la mise en œuvre des différents matériaux. Des casiers pouvant contenir jusqu'à deux mille bouteilles des meilleurs crus sont disposés en forme de U autour d'une salle de dégustation coiffée par une coupole. Le réglage des dispositifs assurant l'éclairage, l'air conditionné et l'ambiance musicale, de même que la gestion des bouteilles en stock, s'effectuent à l'aide d'une simple tablette. Cette cave réalise ainsi une synthèse parfaite entre design haut de gamme, réalisation soignée à base de matériaux de choix et utilisation intelligente de la haute technologie.

Dieses Projekt zeichnet sich durch die leidenschaftliche und intelligente Gestaltung sowie durch einen Entstehungsprozess aus, der in jeder Stufe eine intensive Auseinandersetzung mit der Materie voraussetzte. U-förmig um einen überkuppelten Essbereich angeordnet, beherbergt dieser Weinkeller 2.000 Flaschen seltener und exquisiter Weine. Das Raumklima sowie die Beleuchtung und die Musikanlage lassen sich über ein einziges Tablet steuern, welches zusätzlich über ein ausgeklügeltes System zur Erfassung und Verwaltung der Weine verfügt. Dieser Keller ist die perfekte Mischung aus durchdachtem Design, erlesenstem Handwerk und Materialien sowie den neuesten technischen Möglichkeiten.

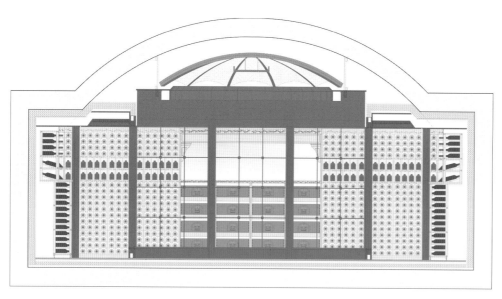

CIRCA RESTAURANT
Memphis, TN, USA

This project is characterized by three screen walls that are arranged in a row facing the pedestrian arcade. Three large wine racks are located behind these screens at a distance of just over a meter. Throughout the design, geometric patterns are carved into the wood, varying from a curvilinear pattern in the dining area to a more rectilinear pattern near the bar. The patterns respond to their function; in the dining area, bottles of wine are stored in a horizontal position where the curved profile creates racks for the bottles. In the bar area, the liquor bottles are displayed in a vertical position and the rectangular incisions create shelves for display. Along the pedestrian arcade, shaded film has been applied to the glass storefront to create varying degrees of privacy.

Cet espace situé à l'intérieur d'une galerie marchande se caractérise par des cloisons en bois ajourées, disposées en ligne à un peu plus d'un mètre devant de grands casiers à bouteilles également en bois. Le concept de décoration utilise aussi bien des lignes courbes que des motifs rectilignes, les différentes formes répondant à des fonctions précises : les courbes permettent de stocker le vin en position horizontale dans la salle de restaurant, tandis que des compartiments rectangulaires servent à entreposer les liqueurs en position verticale derrière le bar. La vitre donnant sur la galerie marchande est pourvue par endroits de film translucide afin de générer des espaces plus intimes.

Drei hohe Trennwände bestimmen den Charakter des Raumes. Sie bilden zusammen eine Reihe, die der Fensterfront an der Fußgängerpassage zugewandt ist. Parallel dazu wurden im Inneren des Restaurants deckenhohe Weinregale installiert. Der gesamte Entwurf basiert auf geometrischen Mustern, die im Restaurantbereich kurvenförmig und in der Nähe der Bar geradlinig verlaufen. Dabei richten sich die Muster nach ihrer jeweiligen Funktion. So bilden sie im Restaurantbereich Regale, in denen Weine liegend gelagert werden können, während sie im Barbereich gerade Flächen zur effektiveren Präsentation der Flaschen erzeugen. Um Zonen mit variierender Privatsphäre zu schaffen, wurde die Glasfront mit Milchglasfolie beklebt.

298

Architect | 3six0 Architecture
Location | 119 South Main Street, Memphis, TN, USA
Year of completion | 2007
Client | John Bragg
Type of venue | hospitality
Number of seating places | 109
Trained sommelier | yes
Storage quality | ★★★☆☆

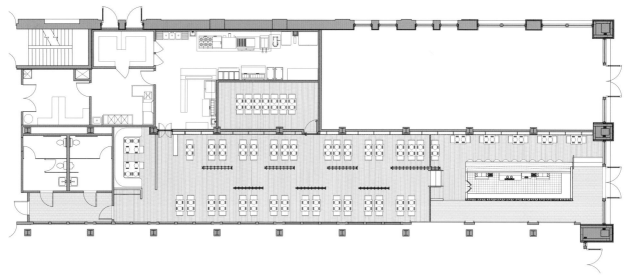

300

INDEX

302

stereoraum Architekten
www.stereoraum.de
244

Architekturbüro Stoppel
www.stoppelarchitekten.de
210

Uxus
www.uxusdesign.com
110

Andreas Weber Architektur + Design,
Barbara Adelmann-Weber
www.andreaswebardesign.de
100, 160

Ignacio Urquiza and Bernardo Quinzaños
CCA I Centro de Colaboración
Arquitectónica
www.cca.mx
214

© Africa Studio / Fotolia.com
136/137, 180/181
AI photography, Prague   66–69
Daniele Ansidei, Berlin   198–201
atelier-f, Fläsch   92 a., b., 94 a. r., b. r.
Marco Alberi Auber   76–81
Dim Balsem, Amsterdam   110–115
Jeremy Bittermann   252–255
Petra Bork / pixelio.de   8
Max Botton   293 a., r.
Filipe Braga   52 b., 54
Zooey Braun   24–27
Andreas Buchberger   190–193
Tamás Bujnovszky, Budapest   164–167
Burg & Schuh, Köln   58–61
José Campos   228–231
CHEck / pixelio.de   10
Alessandra Chemollo
280 a., b. l., 283
Andreas Dengs,
www.photofreaks.ws / pixelio.de   9
Dušan Đorđević
88 a., 90, 91 a. l., r. m., a. r.
Cosmin Dragomir, Bucharest   240–243
Cyrille Druart, Paris   116–119
Andreas Durst   266–269
Cemal Emden, Istanbul   248–251
Ralph Feiner, Malans   262–265
Focus Wine Cellars
16–19, 284–287, 294–297
Klaus Frahm, Berlin   40–43
David Frutos   106–109
Rafael Garno   224 a., 225, 226, 227
Michael Geis   279 a. r.
Group Taillevent, Paris   48–51
Heiko Gruber, Rüdesheim   62–65
Fernando Guerra + Sergio Guerra
52a., 53, 55, 82–87
Tom Gundelwein   274–278
Gerhard Hagen, Bamberg   194–197
Roland Halbe, Stuttgart   20–23, 120–123
Grant Hancock   220–223
John Horner   298–300
Arne Jennard, Antwerp   232–235
Christiane Jeromin   138 b., 139 b., 141 l.
Joe Kesrouani
70 a., 71 b .r., 72, 73 l., 74, 75 b.
Bruno Klomfar   32–35
Andreas Lerchl, Stuttgart   236–239
Patryk Lewiński   142 a., 143 b. r., 144
© Dario Lo Presti / Fotolia.com   104/105
Jorge López-Conde, Madrid   128–131
Duško Marušić   88 b., 89 b. l., b. r.
Hannes Meraner   281 b. l., b. r., 282
Stefan Meyer, Berlin   44–47
Benjamin Miatto   266–269
Hiroshi Mizusaki, Fukuoka   202–205
Molter Linnemann Architekten
206 b., 207 b., 208 l., a. r., b.
Christine Müller   256–261
© natashaphoto / Fotolia.com   56/57

Diego Opazo   12–15
Michal Osmenda / Wikimedia
Commons   6
Dyland Perrenoud   96–99
Michael Peukert, Münchenstein
93 b. l., b. r., 94 l., 95
Marcin Ratajczak
142 b., 143 b. l., 145 a. l., r. m., r. b.
Holger Rathfelder, Stuttgart   182–185
© Alexander Raths / Fotolia.com   218/219
Iris Rothe, Offenburg   100–103
Stefan Ruther   206 a., 207 a., 209
Erick Saillet   288–292, 293 l.
Carles Sala, Barcelona   28–31
Jeremy San, Singapore   156–159
Elke Sawistowski / pixelio.de   11 b.
Rainer Schoditsch, Eisenstadt   270–273
Mark Sengstbratl   172–175
Signa   124–127
sistémica, Mexico City   224 b.
Susanne Sommerfeld, Konstanz
36–39, 168–171
Spitzbart + partners   146–151, 186–189
Ralf Stratmann, Greven   160–163
Dietmar Strauß   210–213, 266–269
twinlili / pixelio.de   11 a.
Estudio Urquiza   214–217
Natalia Vial   132–135
Vinnie Volkerijk
70 b., 71 b. l., 73 r. a., r. m., 75 a.
Mathias Weil, Worms
138 a., 139 a., 140, 141 r. b.
Peter Würmli, Zurich   244–247
Charlie Xia, Shanghai   152–155, 176–179

All other pictures were made available by
the architects and designers.

Cover front: Focus Wine Cellars
Cover back: Signa (left), Filipe Braga
(right)

IMPRINT

The Deutsche Nationalbibliothek lists this publication in the Deutsche Nationalbibliografie; detailed bibliographic data are available in the Internet at http://dnb.dnb.de

ISBN 978-3-03768-183-1
© 2016 by Braun Publishing AG
www.braun-publishing.ch

1st edition 2016
Editor: Editorial Office van Uffelen
Editorial staff and layout: Benjamin Langer, Jessica Metz, Lisa Rogers
Translation: Benjamin Langer, Lisa Rogers, Marcel Saché
Graphic concept: Michaela Prinz, Berlin
Reproduction: Bild1Druck GmbH, Berlin

ACKNOWLEDGMENT

Sommeliers' Heaven started as an original idea from Luca Valeggia and Nicolas Steyaert. Wines deserve a distinctive place to be stored and showcased. They hope that this book can be a source of inspiration for your own personal wine cellaring endeavours.